50 BLACK COUNTRY GHOST STORIES

From Coal Mines to Castles: Eerie Accounts of Black Country Spirits

Lee Brickley

CONTENTS

INTRODUCTION

In a world filled with everyday routines and common sights, there's a hidden side—a place filled with mysterious tales and spooky legends. This hidden place is called the Black Country, and its stories have a strange way of pulling people in. I'm Lee Brickley, a person who loves solving mysteries about ghosts and the unknown, and I come from Cannock, a town close to the Black Country. This region has always felt like a magnet to me, calling me closer with its eerie tales.

I grew up hearing stories about the Black Country, even though I lived just outside of it. Many nights, sitting around fires or huddled in living rooms, I would hear tales that would send shivers down my spine. These weren't just stories to scare or entertain—they felt real. I became curious, wanting to know more. So, I started looking into old books and talking to many people, eager to share their spooky experiences with me.

The Black Country is more than just a name on a map. It's like a giant quilt made up of memories, emotions, and tales from long ago. Imagine a place where the sky sometimes looks as dark as coal and old castles still stand tall. In this place, every stone you step on, every path you walk, and every stream you cross seems to have a story. Some of these stories have been written down, while others have been shared by word of mouth, passed from grandparents to parents to children, becoming scarier with each telling.

Kids often have the wildest stories. Maybe it's because their minds are so open and free. They tell tales of seeing things that grown-ups might not notice or believe. But, it's not just kids who've shared their stories with me. People of all ages have whispered to me about ghostly figures they've seen, mysterious sounds they've heard, and places where it feels like time has stopped or gone all weird.

Now, I invite you on a special journey with me. As you read the stories in this book, try to picture them in your mind. Imagine you see faint shadows moving just out of sight or hear soft songs coming from empty rooms. And maybe, just maybe, you'll feel a cold touch, as if someone from the past is reaching out. As you dive deeper into these tales, always remember: the line between what's real and what's imagined can sometimes become very thin.

And a small piece of advice? Keep a light on while you read. Not just because some of these stories might be a bit scary, but as a reminder that even in the darkest tales, there's always a bit of light shining through. Just be careful—when you look into the mysterious world of the Black Country, it might just look back at you.

So, get ready. There are many secrets waiting for you in the Black Country.

— Lee Brickley

THE MINER'S LAMENT

In the heart of the Black Country, where coal was king and miners toiled beneath the Earth's crust, a story emerged from the depths—one that resonated through time, binding generations in a tale of love, sacrifice, and forewarning.

In the small mining town of Darlaston, 1894, life was simple, yet hard. Families were knit tight, not just by blood but by the shared hardship of mining life. The Jackson family was no different. Samuel, the head of the family, was a miner, just like his father before him and his grandfather before that. It was a legacy of soot-covered faces, strong backs, and the omnipresent danger lurking below.

Samuel's wife, Eleanor, was a strong-willed woman, accustomed to the rigours of mining life. She had seen many families lose their loved ones to the mine's unforgiving embrace and prayed every day that hers would not join those ranks. Their two children, Thomas and Lila, were the apples of their eyes—bright, inquisitive, and full of life.

One particular evening, as the sun began its descent, casting long shadows that played tricks on the eyes, Eleanor found herself feeling more anxious than usual. Samuel hadn't returned from his shift, and the sun was setting—a bad omen in a miner's home.

As night drew closer, a thick fog began to envelop Darlaston. The streets, usually echoing with the sounds of children playing or miners returning home, grew eerily quiet. Eleanor tried to keep her fears at bay, humming an old lullaby as she set the table, hoping to hear the familiar footsteps of her husband at the door.

But the door remained shut.

The hours ticked by, and Eleanor's worry turned to despair. Thomas and Lila, sensing their mother's distress, clung to each other, trying to find solace in their shared unease.

Suddenly, a soft tapping echoed through the silent house. Eleanor, her heart in her throat, approached the front door and hesitated. Taking a deep breath, she opened it slowly.

No one stood there.

But as the fog swirled at her feet, she saw a faint outline—a silhouette, slowly taking form. It was Samuel—or rather, a spectral version of him. His eyes, usually warm and filled with life, were now hollow, and his skin, once ruddy with health, was translucent. He was hovering, his feet never touching the ground.

Frozen in shock, Eleanor could barely muster a voice, but her love for Samuel gave her strength. "Samuel?" she whispered.

His spectral form moved closer, and his voice, though distant, was filled with urgency. "Eleanor," he began, "you must take the children and leave. The mine... it's not safe. There's a deadly gas leak. Warn the town. Save our kin."

Eleanor's heart raced. Fear and sorrow battled within her. "But, Samuel, where are you? Why are you like this?"

His ghostly figure seemed to waver, as if caught between two worlds. "I'm trapped, Eleanor. But you and the children still have a chance. Go, now!"

Wasting no time, Eleanor gathered Thomas and Lila, wrapping them in warm cloaks. Together, they raced through the streets of Darlaston, banging on doors and shouting warnings. Many residents, upon seeing the panic in Eleanor's eyes and hearing the urgency in her voice, heeded her words, evacuating their homes and moving to safer ground.

By morning, Darlaston was alive with the sound of sirens and shouts as rescue operations began at the mine. The news was grim: a catastrophic gas explosion had claimed the lives of many miners, including Samuel.

The town mourned its losses, but thanks to Samuel's spectral warning and Eleanor's swift actions, many more lives were saved.

As the days turned into weeks, and weeks into months, life slowly returned to a semblance of normalcy. But Eleanor and her children never forgot the night Samuel returned from the shadows, guiding them to safety.

In the years that followed, many in Darlaston spoke of "The Miner's Lament"—a testament to love that transcends the veil of life and death. Some say, on foggy nights, you can still see Samuel's ghost wandering the streets, watching over the town and its residents, ensuring their safety from dangers lurking both above and below the ground.

And so, from the dark bowels of the Black Country's mines, a tale of love, loss, and redemption emerged—a tale that would be whispered for generations, serving as both a warning and a testament to the enduring spirit of those who call the Black Country home.

LADY OF DUDLEY CASTLE

Dudley Castle, a grand and imposing structure with a history stretching back centuries, stood atop a hill overlooking the town below. Its battle-worn stones had seen countless seasons come and go, standing testament to triumphs, tragedies, and the unyielding passage of time. But beyond its historical significance, there was a more ethereal presence that clung to the castle—a haunting tale of love and despair.

In the late 1800s, the castle, though aged, was still home to the distinguished Whitmore family. Lord Frederick Whitmore, the current head of the family, was known throughout the region as a just and fair man, ruling over his estate with a combination of firmness and compassion.

However, it was not Lord Frederick but his daughter, Lady Isabella, who was the central figure in our tale. A vision of grace and beauty, with raven-black hair and piercing blue eyes, Lady Isabella was the jewel of Dudley Castle. She was known not just for her looks but also for her kind heart and boundless spirit.

Lady Isabella had a particular fondness for the castle's rose garden—a tranquil space filled with the scent of blooming flowers, the buzz of bees, and the gentle whisper of leaves. It was here she would often retreat to read, daydream, or simply lose herself in the beauty around her.

But one fateful evening, as the sun cast golden hues over the castle grounds, Isabella's sanctuary would become the backdrop for a meeting that would change the course of her life. A young poet named Edmund, having heard tales of the beautiful Lady Isabella, dared to trespass onto the castle grounds in hopes of catching a glimpse of her.

As Isabella strolled among the roses, she was startled by a soft voice reciting a beautiful verse. Following the sound, she came upon Edmund, who, with a sheaf of papers in his hand and a look of sheer awe in his eyes, was composing a poem inspired by her beauty.

Their encounter was brief, but it sparked a romance that would burn brightly yet all too briefly. Secret meetings in the rose garden, whispered promises beneath the starry sky, and stolen moments within the castle's hidden nooks became their world.

Yet, love, as intense as it was, had its adversaries. Lord Frederick, upon discovering his daughter's affair with a commoner, was incensed. He forbade Isabella from ever seeing Edmund again and made plans to marry her off to a duke from a neighbouring town.

Despairing and feeling trapped, Isabella penned a heart-wrenching letter to Edmund, pouring her feelings onto paper. She then decided on a desperate act—she would escape the castle, leaving everything behind, and elope with her true love.

However, fate had other plans.

That very night, as Isabella tried to make her escape, a sudden storm enveloped the castle. Lightning cracked the sky, and thunder rumbled with fury. Isabella, lost and disoriented in the tempest, stumbled and fell from the castle's high walls into the raging waters below.

The next morning, as the storm abated, Dudley Castle woke up to a tragedy. The beautiful Lady Isabella, the heart and soul of the castle, was no more. Her body, battered by the storm, was found at the base of the castle walls, her hand still clutching the letter she had written to Edmund.

The castle was plunged into mourning. Lord Frederick, consumed by guilt and grief, became a recluse, locking himself in his chambers. Edmund, heartbroken by the news, vanished from the town, his poetry turning from love to despair.

But the tale doesn't end here.

Soon after Isabella's tragic demise, strange occurrences began to plague Dudley Castle. Visitors and staff reported seeing a spectral figure of a woman, dressed in flowing white, wandering the castle grounds at night, especially near the rose garden. Soft weeping could be heard, and a ghostly voice would occasionally call out, "Edmund..."

It became clear to the residents of Dudley that Lady Isabella's spirit was restless. Unable to unite with her true love in life, she roamed the castle in death, searching for her lost beloved.

Over the years, many sought to exorcise or communicate with the spirit, hoping to bring her peace. Mediums, clairvoyants, and spiritualists frequented the castle, each attempting to reach the troubled soul. But Lady Isabella's spirit, bound by undying love and overwhelming sorrow, proved impossible to appease.

Today, Dudley Castle remains a popular destination, not just for its historical significance but also for those hoping to catch a glimpse of the tragic Lady of Dudley Castle. Visitors, especially on stormy nights, often report seeing a pale figure wandering the gardens, her soft cries echoing through the centuries, a heartbreaking reminder of a love that even death could not extinguish.

The story of Lady Isabella and her undying love for Edmund has become a legend in the Black Country, a melancholic tale that reminds us of the power of love, the pain of loss, and the mysteries that lie beyond the veil of death.

THE CANAL BOAT APPARITION

The intricate web of canals stretching through the Black Country once pulsed with the vigour of England's thriving industrial age. These liquid highways connected towns, transported coal, and fostered communities. Yet, as day turned to night, an eerie calm would descend upon them. On particularly foggy nights, a spectral presence was said to emerge from the mists.

Situated between Cradley Heath and Darlaston, the quaint hamlet of Larkspur was a place seemingly untouched by time. The canal that flowed through its heart was both a lifeline and a source of countless whispered legends. Among these tales, one stood out—the ghostly narrative of the silent canal boat.

Having recently settled in Larkspur to assist her ageing grandfather, Thomas, Lydia Bennett became increasingly captivated by the village's enigmatic folklore. Grandfather Thomas, a repository of local tales, often spoke of mysterious events, but the story of the phantom barge always intrigued Lydia the most.

Decades prior, so the story went, a barge master named Roland lived in Larkspur. He shared his life with a radiant woman named Eliza. Every morning, as the first light pierced the horizon, they would venture out on their barge, ensuring coal reached even the farthest corners of the Black Country.

One mist-laden evening, as Roland and Eliza journeyed home, a sudden, dense fog ensnared them. The world around became an opaque curtain of white. Despite Roland's familiarity with the canal, he failed to spot a collapsed section up ahead. The barge, laden with coal, met with a submerged obstruction. Within moments, it started sinking, pulling Roland and Eliza into the canal's icy embrace.

The following morning, a pall of sorrow hung over Larkspur. Although a search ensued, Roland and Eliza remained lost to the depths.

From that tragedy arose the whispers. On fog-thick nights, villagers claimed to perceive an ethereal barge, eerily illuminated, sliding gracefully over the water. No crew, no sound, just a silent vessel trailing mystery in its wake. As mysteriously as it would appear, it would retreat back into the fog, leaving no trace of its passage.

Lydia, ever the inquisitive soul, yearned to witness this phenomenon firsthand. Thus, equipped with a lamp and a measure of courage, she awaited the ghostly barge on the foggiest nights by the canal.

Weeks elapsed. Then, one evening, a haunting hum reached Lydia's ears—a melancholic tune sung by a female voice. Emerging from the haze was the illusive apparition: a glowing barge. Drawing nearer, Lydia discerned the vessel's name inscribed on its side: Eliza's Voyage. The singing intensified, exuding a profound sense of loss.

Suddenly, the barge halted, revealing the shadowy figures of a man and woman, entwined in an eternal embrace. They gazed at Lydia, their eyes conveying a blend of love, sorrow, and a desperate plea for remembrance.

But as swiftly as it materialised, the barge dissolved back into the fog, leaving Lydia, lamp aglow, tears glistening, on the canal's edge.

Lydia documented her encounter, and the tale soon became village lore. To some, her experience authenticated long-standing beliefs; to others, it turned myth into reality.

The story of Roland and Eliza, and their ceaseless journey on the Eliza's Voyage, served as a touching testament to love's indomitable spirit.

As years rolled on and Lydia aged, the canals of Larkspur continued to flow, bearing not just coal but tales of yesteryears. And on the foggiest of nights, if you strained your ears, you might still catch the plaintive notes of a love that defied time itself.

THE STOURBRIDGE SPECTER

In the industrious heart of the Black Country, Stourbridge stood out as a beacon of artistry and craftsmanship. Among its myriad landmarks, Hathaway & Sons was a crown jewel, producing glassworks of unparalleled quality. Yet, as is often the case with places steeped in history and tradition, the boundaries between the living and the spectral blurred.

Margaret Fletcher, with dreams bigger than the vast expanses of the Black Country, arrived in Stourbridge with aspirations to immerse herself in the art of glassmaking. With her raven-black hair, bright blue eyes, and a demeanour that melded confidence with curiosity, she was a striking presence in the workshops of Hathaway & Sons.

She was quick to learn, mastering techniques that took others years to grasp. Her superiors and peers were both envious and in awe. However, as days turned into nights and she spent countless hours perfecting her craft, Margaret began hearing whispers—not of her prowess, but of a shadowy figure that lurked near the glassworks during the darkest hours.

"Ever seen the spectre, young Fletcher?" teased Frederick, an old artisan, during one late-night work session.

Margaret, raising an eyebrow, replied, "Specter? Do you mean to spook me with ghost tales?"

Albert, her closest colleague and confidant, leaned in, "It's no mere tale. Many have seen him, especially near the old furnace. They say he's a former craftsman, still tethered to his passion."

Weeks passed, and Margaret's curiosity transformed into an obsession. Every shadow, every unexpected draft, every unexplained noise became a potential sign of the spectral craftsman. And then, one particularly foggy night, she saw him.

As the clock tower announced the midnight hour, the atmosphere in the workshop shifted. The fires in the furnace glowed a shade brighter, and the shadows seemed to dance with an eerie energy. And there, by the old furnace, was a translucent figure. He was dressed in a craftsman's attire, complete with goggles, hovering slightly above the ground, meticulously working on something that shimmered and pulsed with light.

Frozen in place, Margaret watched as the figure, engrossed in his craft, shaped the luminous object into a breathtaking piece of art. Then, with a gesture both graceful and purposeful, he released it, allowing it to float up and vanish into the ether.

Gathering her wits, Margaret approached the spot where the spectre had been. She expected to find nothing but was stunned to discover a delicate glass pendant, glowing faintly and shaped like a heart. Holding it in her hands, a rush of emotions, memories, and feelings coursed through her—love, passion, loss, and a boundless love for the craft.

The next day, Margaret recounted her encounter to the artisans. Frederick, with a solemn expression, spoke up, "That was Edmund Hathaway, the founder. He died tragically, but his spirit remains, forever connected to this place. They say he takes moments of deep emotion, passion, or sorrow and crafts them into tangible memories."

Years rolled by, and the tale of Margaret and the Stourbridge Specter became the stuff of legends. She rose to prominence, her pieces becoming highly sought after, each bearing the signature touch of the spectral lessons she'd learned on that fateful night.

She often said that in the heart of Stourbridge, where fire met artistry, the past wasn't really gone. It lingered, guiding and inspiring, ensuring that the legacy of passion and craft lived on through generations.

And so, in the dance of flames and shadows, the story of the living and the spectral continued, an eternal testament to love, art, and the undying spirit of craftsmanship.

THE PHANTOM TRAIN OF WOLVERHAMPTON

Wolverhampton Station, nestled within the heartbeat of the city, was a fusion of architectural heritage and modern functionality. Its walls echoed the stories of countless souls, with daily commuters hustling through its vast platforms, their minds preoccupied with the events of their day. Amidst the constant thrum of motion, the faint laughter of friends reuniting, the soft murmurs of whispered conversations between lovers, and the continuous digital chimes announcing the arrivals and departures of trains melded into a symphony that captured the essence of an urban twilight.

Nicole, with her deep-set hazel eyes always eager for knowledge, was a university student studying history. She was keen on piecing together the past and understanding its correlation with the present. She stood on Platform 3, her gaze occasionally drifting over her textbooks, waiting for her regular evening train. Beside her stood Ryan, her childhood friend and confidant, engrossed in a spirited discussion about their latest lecture on Victorian England.

While Ryan animatedly shared his thoughts, Nicole's attention was diverted to the electronic timetable overhead. Among the list of destinations and their corresponding times was a peculiar listing - the 9:15 to "Nowhere." She blinked, rubbing her eyes to make sure she wasn't seeing things.

Jokingly, she elbowed Ryan, pointing towards the anomalous listing, expecting him to laugh it off as a glitch or some tech enthusiast's idea of a prank. Ryan, always intrigued by tech anomalies, quickly fished out his sleek smartphone, adjusting the lens to snap a picture of the curious entry. However, before he could do so, a sound unfamiliar to the modern ears of the station's inhabitants resonated through the area—a deep, mournful whistle that seemed to echo from a time long past.

Both Nicole and Ryan, along with several other commuters, turned their attention down the tracks. Their collective breaths caught as they saw an approaching spectacle; not one of the streamlined electric trains they were accustomed to, but a grand, majestic steam engine that seemed to have rolled straight out of history. Its metallic body gleamed under the station's fluorescent lights, creating an eerie luminescence that made it appear otherworldly. Its windows revealed fleeting glimpses of passengers—shadowy figures dressed in apparel reminiscent of the late 19th century. Men in sharp suits and bowler hats, women in flowing gowns with lace parasols, and children holding onto handcrafted toys.

The platform's atmosphere grew dense with anticipation and an inexplicable chill. As the spectral train pulled to a gentle stop, doors creaked open, releasing a cold mist that danced around the feet of the stunned onlookers. The distinct aroma of burning coal mingled with the scent of aged leather and polished wood, adding to the train's enigmatic presence.

Among the crowd, an elderly gentleman named Albert, his face etched with lines of age and wisdom, leaned in to share an old tale with a group of intrigued teenagers. "My grandfather once spoke of the ghost train," he began in hushed tones, "a train from yesteryears that reappears every so often, bearing with it the memories of a tragic accident from over a century ago."

Despite the technological age they lived in, none of the commuters' phones or cameras seemed to work in that particular moment. Each time they tried to capture the apparition, their devices malfunctioned or displayed nothing but blank screens. The announcement for the regular 9:20

train to Birmingham jolted the crowd back to reality, and just as mysteriously as it had appeared, the phantom train's doors closed, its whistle gave a final mournful cry, and it receded into the enveloping mist.

The next day, whispers spread throughout Wolverhampton about the ghost train. Although there was no tangible evidence, the shared experience of the eyewitnesses made the tale all the more intriguing. Theories abounded: was it a shared hallucination? A trick of the light? Or a genuine spectral phenomenon?

Months passed, and while the rest of the world continued in its usual rhythm, those present on that fateful evening would always carry the memory of the time they witnessed something inexplicable, something that challenged their understanding of reality. Every visit to the station, every wait on Platform 3, became a reminder that some mysteries are best left unsolved, their magic lying in the unknown.

HALESOWEN HAUNTINGS

The town of Halesowen, nestled in the heart of the Black Country, was home to many whispered tales. But none was as whispered, nor as fiercely debated, as the story of Corridor House. The tall, imposing structure stood alone on Malt Mill Lane, its once pristine brick now darkened by age and neglect, the gardens overrun with bramble and thorn. While Halesowen had its fair share of eerie tales, Corridor House was the town's best-kept secret.

Lillian, an investigative journalist, returned to Halesowen after being away for over a decade. She had fond memories of her childhood, playing in the fields and listening to the elders spin tales of yore. But she also remembered the forbidden allure of Corridor House, the place children were warned away from, lest they rouse the spirits that dwelled within. As a child, she had never ventured near it, but now, with the boldness of adulthood and a thirst for a good story, she decided to unravel the mysteries of the haunted mansion.

Corridor House was so named because of its seemingly endless hallways and passages, doors that led to nowhere, and staircases that circled back on themselves. Rumour had it that it was built by an eccentric architect named Edmund Gravely in the late 1800s. Gravely, a recluse, was said to have designed the house as a sanctuary for the restless spirits of Halesowen, from monks who had lost their way to mill workers whose lives were cut short by tragedy. The townsfolk whispered that the house was both a blessing and a curse—while it kept the spirits contained, it also trapped them, making their anguish palpable to anyone who dared to enter.

Armed with her notebook and camera, Lillian approached the mansion on a crisp autumn morning. As she pushed open the creaking gates, she couldn't help but feel a pang of unease. The air grew colder as she neared the entrance. Determined, she stepped inside, and the musty scent of aged wood and forgotten memories met her. She began to explore, every creak of the floorboards echoing in the cavernous space.

In a hallway lined with portraits, she felt a presence. As she walked, the eyes of the portraits seemed to follow her, their expressions shifting ever so subtly. One particular portrait caught her attention—a beautiful woman in mill attire, her eyes filled with sorrow. The nameplate read "Eleanor." Lillian felt a connection, an inexplicable pull towards the portrait. As she reached out to touch it, a cold hand clasped hers. Startled, she whipped around to find a translucent figure, a woman, who bore a striking resemblance to the portrait.

Eleanor, as Lillian would come to know her, had been a mill worker who fell in love with a monk from the town's monastery. Their forbidden love had been the talk of the town, and one fateful night, they decided to elope. However, tragedy struck. The monk was discovered by his brethren and taken away, while Eleanor, heartbroken, took her life in Corridor House.

The spirit of Eleanor led Lillian through the winding hallways, revealing rooms that housed other spirits—each with their own tragic tale. In one room, Lillian saw monks, forever frozen in prayer, their chants echoing softly. In another, she found children, victims of a mill fire, laughing and playing, unaware of their spectral existence.

But the heart of the house, Eleanor revealed, was the grand ballroom. Here, spirits from all walks of life came together, dancing eternally to a haunting melody played by a phantom orchestra. Lillian watched, both enthralled and horrified, as Eleanor joined the dance, her figure merging with the swirling mass of spirits.

Hours seemed to pass in mere moments, and when Lillian finally made her way out of Corridor House, the sun was setting, casting an orange hue on the forsaken structure. She had her story, but it was one she could never share, for who would believe her?

Days turned into weeks, and Lillian couldn't shake off the experience. She would often find herself drawn back to the mansion, where she would sit by Eleanor's portrait, offering silent company to the spirit that had once been so full of life.

The tale of Corridor House remained Halesowen's best-kept secret, a silent witness to the town's many souls who had once walked its streets, laughed, cried, loved, and lost. And while the world outside moved on, within its walls, the dance of spirits continued, a poignant reminder of lives once lived and the memories they left behind.

THE CRYING CHILD OF WEDNESBURY

In the narrow cobblestone streets of Wednesbury, an old town steeped in history, few dared to tread the maze of alleyways after nightfall. For in the darkness, between the looming brick walls and beneath the pale moonlight, echoed the heart-rending cries of a child—a lost little girl named Clara, separated from her mother by time and tragedy.

In the late 1800s, Wednesbury was bustling with factories and workshops. The Industrial Revolution had brought both prosperity and poverty to the town. Amidst this backdrop lived Margaret, a young widow with her daughter Clara. Life was harsh; Margaret toiled long hours at the local ironworks, and Clara, barely seven, was left to her own devices, often wandering the streets and alleys, waiting for her mother's return.

One evening, as the sun dipped beneath the horizon and Wednesbury was blanketed in a thick fog, Clara, clutching her ragdoll, set out to look for her mother. She ventured further than she ever had before, drawn by the faint hum of the factories. As the hours ticked by, the little girl lost her way in the maze of alleyways. Her calls for her mother went unanswered, and by morning, Clara was nowhere to be found.

Search parties were dispatched, and the townsfolk scoured every nook and cranny, but Clara remained elusive. It was as if the fog had swallowed her whole. Days turned into weeks, and with no sign of Clara, hope dwindled. The only trace of her was the haunting cries that began to echo through the alleyways, a mournful plea for her mother.

Margaret was inconsolable. Every evening, she would walk the alleyways, calling out to Clara, lighting lanterns, and leaving them at various corners, hoping her daughter would find her way back. But as the years passed, and Margaret grew old, she was never reunited with Clara. Broken-hearted, she eventually passed away, but her legacy—a lit lantern outside her home—remained, a beacon for her lost child.

Fast forward to the 1960s, and Wednesbury had evolved. Factories gave way to offices, horse carts to cars, but the alleys, largely unchanged, still echoed with Clara's cries. Tales of the crying child became legend, with many claiming to have seen a little girl in period clothing, clutching a ragdoll, wandering the streets.

Among the town's newer residents was Amelia, a young teacher with a keen interest in local history. Intrigued by the legend, she decided to delve deeper. As she combed through old records, newspaper clippings, and personal diaries, the story of Clara and Margaret came to light. The tragedy touched Amelia deeply, and she felt a compelling need to help.

One foggy evening, reminiscent of that fateful night over a century ago, Amelia ventured into the alleys. Armed with a lantern, she began her search. Hours seemed to blur, the fog growing thicker, the night deeper. Just as Amelia was about to give up, she heard it—a soft whimper, followed by a plaintive cry.

Following the sound, Amelia found herself in front of Margaret's old home, the lantern outside still lit. As she approached, a figure materialised from the fog—a little girl, her dress faded, clutching a tattered ragdoll.

Amelia, without fear, knelt beside Clara, gently took her hand, and whispered words of comfort. She spoke of Margaret's love, her endless search, and the lantern that still shone brightly for her. As the night gave way to dawn, the alleyways were filled with a luminous glow, and Clara's cries grew softer, more peaceful, until they were no more.

Amelia, feeling an overwhelming sense of relief, made her way back home. The townsfolk, upon hearing of her encounter, were astounded. The crying child of Wednesbury, after all these years, had found solace.

To this day, while the cries have ceased, on foggy nights, residents sometimes spot a lone figure—a young teacher with a lantern, walking hand in hand with a little girl, guiding her through the maze of alleyways, ensuring she's never lost again.

BILSTON'S BEWITCHING HOUR

Bilston, with its rich industrial heritage, had its share of legends and folklore. Yet, one story stood out above the rest: the enigmatic events of October 12th, known by locals as the Bewitching Hour.

As the tale went, every year on this date, at precisely midnight, Bilston experienced peculiar occurrences for one hour: candles would relight after being snuffed out, clocks would chime out of sync, and shadows would dance without a source. No one knew why these strange events took place, but the older residents whispered of a pact, an old debt, and the power of four.

In the late 1800s, Bilston thrived due to its coal mines. Among its residents were four close friends - Bob, Sid, John, and Colin. All worked at the same mine and were known to share not only the toils of their labour but also a deep interest in the occult. One evening, in an attempt to contact the other side and perhaps gain insights into their futures, they conducted a séance.

The ritual seemed to be in vain, with no signs or messages from the beyond. Disappointed, the friends went their separate ways. But unbeknownst to them, they had opened a doorway that night.

October 12th, just days after the séance, brought with it the first Bewitching Hour. The four friends, realising their grave mistake, sought to close the rift they had unwittingly created. But despite their efforts, they only managed to strike a deal with the spirits. The town would face the uncanny events of the Bewitching Hour annually, but no harm would come to its residents. However, a price had to be paid: the spirits demanded a guardian, one of the four friends, to ensure the pact was upheld.

The duty rotated among them each year. As the guardian, they would have to wander the streets of Bilston during the Bewitching Hour, ensuring no one was outside and that the spirits' antics remained harmless. If any resident was harmed or if the guardian himself failed to be outside during the Bewitching Hour, the pact would be broken, and Bilston would be at the mercy of restless spirits.

The friends kept their secret, fulfilling their roles as guardians till their last breaths. As years turned into decades, the origins of the Bewitching Hour became a mystery, its truth known only in hushed tales among the eldest in Bilston.

Fast forward to the 1950s. The Bewitching Hour had become a local legend, with most treating it as a quirky anomaly. However, the elderly still locked their doors and stayed indoors, passing on warnings to younger generations.

Enter James, a young journalist, and a sceptic, who had recently moved to Bilston. Fascinated by the tale, he decided to investigate. His inquiries led him to an ancient diary at the local library, detailing the events involving Bob, Sid, John, and Colin. The journal ended with a dire warning about the pact and the importance of the guardian.

Realising that the last of the original guardians had passed away years ago, James grew anxious. Who was the guardian now? Was Bilston unprotected? Determined to witness the Bewitching Hour himself, he decided to stay out on the upcoming October 12th.

As midnight approached, James positioned himself in the town square. The air grew cold, and an eerie silence enveloped Bilston. Suddenly, the peculiarities began—clocks chimed, shadows danced, and an unsettling feeling of being watched prevailed.

To James's surprise, an old figure emerged from the fog, walking slowly with a lantern. It was old man Thompson, known to be a descendant of one of the four friends. As they locked eyes, Thompson beckoned James over, sharing the tale of his lineage and his inherited duty as the guardian.

James, realising the gravity of the situation and the danger Bilston could face without a guardian, offered to help. Thompson, knowing his time was limited, gratefully accepted, training James in the ways of the guardian.

For years, under Thompson's guidance, James upheld the tradition, wandering the streets of Bilston every October 12th. The Bewitching Hour, while still mysterious, remained harmless under his watchful eye.

As the years went by and modernity swept through Bilston, the Bewitching Hour became a celebrated event. Locals would gather indoors, sharing tales and awaiting the chimes at midnight, while outside, the guardian, a role now passed down through generations, would patrol the streets, ensuring the safety of the town and the continuation of a pact made over a century ago.

And so, in the heart of the Black Country, in the town of Bilston, a legend persisted—a testament to the bond of four friends, a debt to the spirit world, and the ever-watchful guardian of the Bewitching Hour.

THE WEST BROMWICH WANDERER

West Bromwich, a town of rich history, had been shaped and scarred by the events of the past. Among its many stories, one remained particularly poignant, of a soldier named Danny who, even in death, had never truly left.

The early 20th century saw the world embroiled in a devastating war. Young men from West Bromwich, filled with patriotic fervour, joined the ranks, heading off to distant lands with dreams of valour and heroism. Danny was among them, a passionate young man with a love for music, especially the drums. He was quickly assigned as a drummer for his battalion, responsible for setting the marching beat.

Back home, Danny left behind a grieving mother, Mary, a younger brother, Ron, and Vera, the love of his life. They exchanged letters, finding solace in written words amidst the chaos of war. Vera cherished Danny's letters, where he often mentioned the rhythm of his drum, a beat that helped him push forward, a beat that he hoped would lead him back home to her.

As the war raged on, news from the frontlines brought tales of despair and loss. Then, one fateful day, a letter arrived at Mary's residence, bearing the tragic news of Danny's demise. He had been caught in a surprise ambush, and amidst the firefight, his comrades recalled hearing the haunting beats of his drum till the very end.

The town mourned their lost hero. Vera, heartbroken, could never find closure. She would visit the local churchyard, sitting beside Danny's memorial, whispering words of love and longing.

Months turned into years, and a peculiar tale began to circulate in West Bromwich. On foggy nights, a rhythmic drumbeat echoed through the streets, starting softly, growing louder, then fading away. Those who claimed to have heard it described an otherworldly sound, simultaneously comforting and eerie.

As the sightings increased, so did the stories. People spoke of a shadowy figure marching through the mist, a soldier with a drum, his steps synchronised to its beat. The apparition was soon christened "The West Bromwich Wanderer."

Vera, having heard the tales, ventured out one fog-laden night. As midnight approached, she began to hear it—the familiar beat of Danny's drum. Drawn to it, she followed the sound until she reached the old town square. There, she saw him, a spectral figure, holding a drum. Their eyes met, and for a brief moment, the weight of time and sorrow lifted. Danny's spirit marched past her, his eternal beat fading into the distance. Vera, tears streaming down her face, felt a peace she hadn't felt in years. She believed that Danny's love, strong and undying, had brought him back, marching forevermore in the streets of West Bromwich.

Ron, Danny's younger brother, now in his twenties, was initially sceptical of the tales. However, a chance encounter changed his perspective. One evening, while walking home, he too heard the rhythmic beats. Looking around, he saw the ghostly figure of a soldier—his brother, Danny. Ron, overcome with emotion, attempted to approach him, but the figure continued its march, never breaking stride, disappearing into the mist. Ron later confided in Vera, and they found solace in their shared experiences.

Years rolled on, and the story of The West Bromwich Wanderer became an integral part of town lore. Locals would gather on foggy nights, hoping to catch a glimpse or hear the distant beats. Children grew up hearing the romantic tale of the soldier who marches eternally for love.

Elders like Vera and Ron, now in their twilight years, became the custodians of Danny's story, ensuring that the legend lived on. They organised annual remembrance marches on the day of Danny's passing, where townsfolk would march to the rhythm of a drum, honouring the memory of their ghostly soldier.

The story, while haunting, became a symbol of enduring love and sacrifice for West Bromwich. It reminded the town of the price of war, the souls lost, and the echoes that remain. In the heart of the Black Country, amidst tales of spectres and apparitions, the rhythmic beat of The West Bromwich Wanderer's drum resonated the loudest, a testament to a love that defied even death.

ROWLEY REGIS RAPPINGS

Rowley Regis, with its undulating hills and historic charm, was a desirable place for families seeking peace away from the bustling urban life. The Woodcroft farmhouse, standing proud on a knoll overlooking the town, had been a part of the landscape for centuries. With its dark wooden beams and stone foundation, it held the secrets of generations.

In the autumn of 1892, Cindy and her daughter Kelly moved into the farmhouse. They were in search of a fresh start following the tragic demise of Mr. Woodcroft, Cindy's husband and Kelly's father. The sprawling fields and quiet surroundings seemed perfect, offering solace and healing.

However, soon after settling in, the house began revealing its peculiarities. The first incident occurred on a windless night when Kelly, nestled in her bed, heard a soft rap on her window pane. Thinking it a tree branch or an animal, she paid it no mind. Yet, the rapping grew more insistent, following a rhythmic pattern: three raps, a pause, then two more.

Startled, Kelly called out for her mother. Cindy, having heard the noise herself, came rushing in. Together, they looked out the window, but the moonlit yard revealed nothing. They attributed the noise to their tired minds and tried to put it behind them.

However, as days turned into weeks, the rappings became a nightly occurrence, not limited to just Kelly's window. Sometimes, they echoed from the walls, the attic, or even the floorboards beneath. But every time, the pattern remained the same: three raps, a pause, then two more.

Concerned, Cindy sought help from the local villagers. Many

were hesitant to speak of it, offering only sympathetic looks and vague warnings. But an elderly woman, Mrs. Thompson, shared a tale that sent shivers down Cindy's spine.

Many years ago, when the farmhouse was newly built, it was occupied by a young couple deeply in love. However, their love story was tragically cut short when the husband, a soldier, was called to war. Before leaving, they created a secret code to communicate in case he was ever in danger and needed to send her a covert message: three raps, a pause, and then two more, which stood for "I love you."

The husband was captured and held in a prisoner-of-war camp. One night, a fellow prisoner, an old man gifted in the arcane arts, offered him a chance to send a message to his beloved wife. Using a ritual, the husband sent his coded message of love through the veil of realms.

Back at the farmhouse, his wife heard the rapping. Recognizing the code, she was filled with both joy and dread. Overcome with emotion, she fell gravely ill and passed away, her heart broken from the weight of love and despair.

Cindy listened, her heart heavy, wondering if she had unknowingly disturbed the spirits with her own grief. Determined to find peace for both the spirit and her family, she decided to hold a séance with Kelly and Mrs. Thompson's assistance.

On the chosen night, with candles lit and a circle of salt drawn, the trio sat around a table, hands joined. Cindy spoke gently, acknowledging the spirit and its message of love. She assured it that its message had been heard and asked it to find peace, to reunite with its loved one in the realm beyond.

A heavy silence enveloped the room. Then, the familiar rapping began, but this time, it sounded different—gentler, almost grateful. Three raps, a pause, then two more. The candles flickered, and a gust of wind blew through the room, extinguishing them.

When the lights were relit, an air of calmness filled the farmhouse. The oppressive weight that once hung in the air had lifted. The rappings, which had once terrorised Cindy and Kelly, had ceased.

Years passed, and the Woodcroft farmhouse saw many more occupants, but the rappings were never heard again. The story of that fateful séance became a part of Rowley Regis lore, a tale of love transcending realms and the power of understanding and compassion.

Cindy and Kelly, having confronted the spectre of their past, found peace in the farmhouse, turning it into a home filled with love and laughter. The Rowley Regis Rappings became a testament to the town's rich history, a tale whispered on dark nights, reminding all of the enduring power of love and the mysteries that lay just beyond the veil of the known.

TIPTON'S TOLL HOUSE TERROR

Tipton, a town well-known for its canals and industrial past, was also home to a historic toll house – an edifice that bore witness to countless travellers, goods, and stories. With arched windows and a cobblestone path, the tollhouse was a picture of quaintness, standing as a testament to a bygone era. Yet, for all its charm, there was an enigma surrounding it – an old tale, spoken of only in hushed tones, called the 'Tollhouse Terror'.

In the summer of 1910, Jane and her son Oscar, who were travelling writers, decided to visit Tipton to document its history and legends. Having heard whispers of the tollhouse, they decided to lodge there for a week, hoping to experience and chronicle the local lore.

Upon their arrival, Mr. Smith, the elderly innkeeper, welcomed them warmly. The toll house, having been converted into an inn, retained much of its historic charm with antique furnishings and faded photographs of bygone days.

On their first evening, while dining in the candlelit common room, Jane inquired about the tale of the 'Tollhouse Terror'. Mr. Smith, after a moment's hesitation, began his tale.

Years ago, when the toll house was still operational, a tollkeeper named Michael managed it. His duty was to collect the fees from travellers using the road. However, Michael was not just satisfied with monetary payments. He was a greedy man and often demanded personal items or keepsakes, especially if he deemed them valuable. Many a traveller had to part with cherished items to continue their journey.

One fateful night, a hooded traveller approached, carrying nothing but a small ornate box. When Michael demanded it as toll, the traveller warned him that the box was not to be opened and that its contents were not meant for the greedy. Blinded by curiosity and avarice, Michael scoffed and snatched the box, allowing the traveller to pass.

That night, Michael's greed got the better of him, and he opened the box. No one knows what he saw, but his screams echoed throughout Tipton. The next morning, the townsfolk found the tollhouse deserted. All that remained was the open box and Michael's cap. He was never seen again. Since then, it is said that his spirit lingers, demanding a different kind of toll from those who stay – a token of their most treasured memories.

Jane and Oscar listened with rapt attention, a chill running down their spines. Yet, being rational thinkers, they took the story as a mere tale meant to spook visitors.

That night, as the mother and son duo settled into their rooms, a cold wind blew, making the candles flicker. In the dead of the night, Oscar was awakened by a faint tapping on his door. Thinking it was his mother, he opened it to find the corridor empty. But on the floor lay a worn-out cap – resembling the one Mr. Smith had mentioned.

Startled, he rushed to his mother's room. Jane, looking pale, confessed to hearing whispered demands for a "treasured memory" in her dreams. They both felt an unseen presence, an oppressive weight in the air, a silent demand for payment.

Realising that they might have stirred the spirit of Michael, they decided to offer something of personal value, hoping to appease him. Jane, taking out a locket containing a picture of her late husband, placed it on the table in the common room with a note expressing their intent. Oscar, on the other hand, penned down a cherished childhood memory and left it alongside.

As dawn approached, the oppressive atmosphere began to lift. The mother and son, though shaken, felt a certain calmness enveloping the tollhouse. The next morning, they found their offerings untouched but felt an inexplicable emptiness, a sense of loss, as if a memory had been plucked from their minds.

Recognizing the gravity of the tollhouse's legend, they decided to cut their stay short. Before leaving, they narrated their experience to Mr. Smith, who listened with a sombre nod. He then handed them a guestbook, urging them to pen down their experience as a warning for future lodgers.

Years rolled on, and the legend of the 'Tollhouse Terror' grew. While many deemed it a mere tale, those who'd stayed at the tollhouse and paid Michael's unique toll knew of its haunting reality.

Jane and Oscar's writings on Tipton, including their eerie encounter at the tollhouse, were eventually published, earning them acclaim. However, the tollhouse chapter always bore a postscript: "Some tolls, though not monetary, exact a far greater price. Beware the demands of memories lost."

The toll house, while still standing, became a place of reverence and caution – a reminder of the town's rich history, interwoven with tales of avarice, retribution, and the inexorable demands of the 'Tollhouse Terror'.

SMETHWICK'S SILENT BELL

In the heart of the Black Country, the town of Smethwick bore its industrial heritage like a badge of honour. Its streets echoed stories of generations past, but none so hauntingly melancholic as the tale of the Silent Bell of St. Margaret's Church.

On the eve of every 15th of November, an eerie phenomenon would grip the town. St. Margaret's Church bell, under the shroud of night, would ring out a sombre melody. No human hand touched it, no mechanism set it into motion; it tolled of its own accord, ringing with a sadness that resonated through the very bones of Smethwick.

The origins of this spectral occurrence traced back a century. Reece, a young and enthusiastic lad, was the church's bell ringer. The boy had a gift; his fingers danced on the ropes, making the bells sing melodies that filled the air with joy. On any festive occasion or celebration, the townsfolk would eagerly await Reece's tunes, which brought life to their events.

However, tragedy has a cruel way of silencing joy. One fateful evening, on the 15th of November, as Reece was engrossed in a particularly challenging tune, he lost his footing and met a tragic end in the bell tower. The town was consumed by grief. The lively melodies that once graced their celebrations were now a painful reminder of the loss of their beloved bell ringer.

The following year, on the anniversary of Reece's untimely death, as the clock struck midnight, the residents of Smethwick were startled awake. The church bell was ringing, not in its usual rhythmic pattern, but in a melancholic tune. Those brave enough rushed to the church, only to find the bell tower empty, with the ropes untouched.

Father David, a young priest at St. Margaret's at the time, was one of the witnesses. He recognized the tune immediately - it was the same one Reece was attempting on that tragic night. Year after year, the phenomenon repeated, with the bell tolling its mournful song on the same date, at the same time.

Peter, a local schoolteacher and an enthusiast of local legends, had grown up hearing the tale. This year, along with his friend Oscar, he decided to stay in the church on the eve of the 15th, hoping to experience the legend firsthand. They camped in the church, setting up chairs to have a clear view of the bell tower.

Night deepened, and the hours passed in hushed anticipation. Father David joined them, lighting candles and reciting prayers in Reece's memory. As the clock hands inched toward midnight, a heavy silence descended.

And then, it began. The bell tolled its haunting song. The melody, filled with longing and sorrow, echoed through the church and into the streets of Smethwick. Peter, Oscar, and Father David sat transfixed, each lost in the depths of the poignant sound.

Once the last note faded into the cold night, the trio made their way to the bell tower, only to confirm what they already knew – no one had been there. The ropes were still, untouched by any hand.

In the days that followed, the story of the Silent Bell was on everyone's lips. The older residents nodded knowingly, having experienced the spectral event in their youth, while the younger ones listened wide-eyed, a mix of scepticism and awe evident on their faces.

Every year, the townsfolk of Smethwick would gather at St. Margaret's on the 15th of November, lighting candles in memory of Reece and hoping to hear the spectral melody of the Silent Bell. It became a solemn event, a night of remembrance, not just for Reece, but for all those who had passed away, leaving behind stories that would echo through time.

The Silent Bell of Smethwick, with its mournful tune, stood as a testament to the town's rich history, a bridge between the living and the dead, reminding everyone that some stories, some memories, never truly fade away.

THE SHADOW OF SANDWELL VALLEY

Nestled within the heart of the Black Country, Sandwell Valley provided a natural respite from the industrialised surroundings. A lush green expanse, it beckoned nature lovers, hikers, and families looking for a quiet day in the great outdoors. Its scenic trails, dense woods, and serene lakes had been witness to countless laughter, joyous picnics, and adventurous treks. But as the dusk approached and shadows lengthened, a different tale emerged, whispered among the locals - a tale of an elusive shadow that trailed behind the unsuspecting.

Kevin, an avid hiker, had heard the murmurs of the mysterious shadow but had brushed them off as local myths meant to scare children. However, one evening changed his perspective forever.

He and his friends, Sandra and Bobby, decided to venture on a late afternoon hike through the valley. Their plan was to reach the other end by evening and camp out. They packed their gear, laced their boots, and embarked on their journey with enthusiasm.

The day began beautifully. The sun shone brightly, casting a golden hue on the trail. Birds sang, and the gentle rustling of leaves underfoot accompanied their every step. Hours flew by as they trekked, with occasional stops to admire the scenic beauty or to share a light joke.

However, as the sun started to dip below the horizon, an unexpected chill descended upon Sandwell Valley. Kevin, sensing a sudden drop in temperature, pulled his jacket tighter around him. Sandra, usually cheerful and full of stories, grew silent, her eyes darting nervously around the woods.

Bobby, attempting to lighten the mood, teased, "Getting scared, are we? Afraid of the legendary Sandwell Shadow?"

Kevin chuckled, but Sandra shot them both a concerned look. "I don't know," she whispered, "but I feel like we're not alone."

The path ahead, which once seemed welcoming, now appeared ominous. The towering trees seemed to close in, and every rustle, every whisper of the wind, set their nerves on edge. They increased their pace, eager to reach their campsite.

As the twilight deepened, Sandra suddenly halted, her eyes fixed on the path behind them. "Do you see that?" she breathed, pointing at a vague silhouette that seemed to flit between the trees, always just out of clear sight.

Kevin squinted, trying to make out what Sandra was pointing at. There it was – a shadowy figure, neither fully human nor entirely formless, moving silently but staying consistently behind them. It didn't approach but didn't recede either.

Bobby gulped. "The Sandwell Shadow..." he whispered, realisation dawning.

With their hearts pounding, the trio decided to stick close. They abandoned their idea of camping and focused solely on exiting the valley as quickly as possible. But the shadow persisted, maintaining its distance, an eerie presence always in their periphery.

Every so often, they would hear faint murmurs, incomprehensible whispers that seemed to be carried by the wind. Once, Sandra thought she heard a lament, a sorrowful cry that seemed to echo the valley's ancient woes.

The path, which had been clear during the day, seemed to twist and turn unpredictably under the cloak of darkness. Every shadowed corner, every rustling bush added to their growing dread.

Hours that felt like an eternity passed. Their once energetic strides were now hurried, desperate steps. But as they neared the valley's exit, the oppressive feeling started to lift. The whispers grew fainter, the temperature rose, and the lurking shadow began to fade.

Stepping out of Sandwell Valley, the trio heaved a sigh of relief. The bustling streets of the Black Country seemed exceptionally welcoming that night. They promised each other never to venture into the valley after dusk again.

Word of their eerie encounter spread. Some dismissed it as an effect of the dimming light or an overactive imagination. But those who had experienced the shadowy presence knew the truth. Over time, the legend of the Sandwell Valley Shadow grew. Parents warned their children, and hikers ensured they left the valley before nightfall.

Sandra, Kevin, and Bobby went on many more adventures together, but none ever matched the haunting experience of that evening in Sandwell Valley. While they never spoke of it openly, the memory remained etched in their minds, a chilling reminder of the time they were trailed by the enigmatic shadow of Sandwell Valley.

THE IRONWORKER'S RETURN

Kyle's footsteps resonated against the cobbled pathways of his beloved Black Country, echoing amidst the soft, eerie whispers of the winds that rustled through the autumnal leaves. A descendant of hardy folk who'd forged their legacies amidst fires and anvil, whose sweat and toil had given life to the iron and steel that now lay as silent relics of an illustrious past.

The streets of Black Country, imbued with industrial affluence and the stoic spirit of its people, bore silent testimonies to an era where iron and steel reigned supreme. Amidst the silent chimneys and dormant forges, where once the roar of fires and clang of hammers permeated the air, now lay a solemn silence; a silence as profound as the annals of history that resided within the depths of its foundations.

Kyle was no stranger to the tales of old. Narratives of spectral presences, haunting echoes, and ethereal entities were woven into the fabric of his existence. Yet amongst them all, the tale of the Ironworker's Return was whispered in hushed tones, a narrative as enigmatic as the silent, moonlit nights.

On one such moonlit night, where the silvery luminescence cast eerie shadows that danced amidst the silent structures, Kyle found himself inexplicably drawn towards the old ironworks. A place where legends spoke of a spectre, an ironworker of yore, whose soul was said to be forever bonded with the silent machinery.

As Kyle ambled through the silent pathways, the soft murmurs of the wind weaving through the dormant chimneys resonated with haunting melodies of the past. The ironworks, though silent, whispered tales of the illustrious past, echoing the grandeur and tragedies that lay within its silent walls.

The rusted gears and silent conveyors bore the imprints of diligent hands, hands that had toiled amidst fire and steel, forging legacies that now stood as silent monuments. It was amidst this haunting silence, where the boundaries between the earthly and ethereal seemed to dissolve, that Kyle encountered the spectral entity.

A figure, clad in the garbs of an era long past, his presence echoing the haunting rhythms of the old world. In his hands, a hammer struck against the anvil, illuminating the silent corridors with ethereal sparks that danced amidst the shadows. The ghostly ironworker was engaged in eternal labour, his soul forever weaving the haunting symphony of iron and steel.

Every strike of the hammer echoed the tales of human aspirations and earthly tragedies. The ghostly flames of the furnace illuminated a spectral dance, casting eerie reflections that danced amidst the silent machinery and rusted gears.

Kyle, entranced by the haunting spectacle, stood amidst the eerie dance of light and shadow. The ironworker, oblivious to his presence, was immersed in his eternal toil, each strike of the hammer resonating with the silent sorrows and unfulfilled aspirations of a life untimely claimed.

The old tales whispered of an ambitious worker, diligent and dedicated, who'd met a tragic demise, his soul forever bound to the spectral machinery, his aspirations echoing in the haunting rhythms of the ghostly hammer.

Kyle felt a profound connection with the spectral entity. Every ethereal spark, every haunting echo, resonated with the silent tales that lay embedded in the soul of the Black Country. As the first rays of dawn kissed the silent edifice, the ghostly figure faded into the ethereal embrace, the clanks of the hammer dissolving into the silent whispers of the awakening world.

The experience, though unspeakable, was imprinted in Kyle's soul. The old ironworks, with its silent machinery and haunting echoes, bore the imprints of lives and legacies that transcended the corporeal existence.

Kyle ventured back into the world of the living, the silent corridors, the ghostly flames, and the spectral ironworker forever etched in his memory. In the silent nights, when the moon cast its eerie glow upon the silent chimneys and dormant forges, he would find himself drawn towards the old ironworks.

A silent witness to the eternal dance of souls that echoed the untold tales and unsung melodies of the illustrious past. In the haunting embrace of the Black Country, where the past and present, the living and dead, danced amidst the silent structures and eerie pathways, the legend of the Ironworker's Return was silently whispered, a haunting narrative as enigmatic as the silent, moonlit nights.

THE WALSALL WRAITH

Suzanne and Cheryl were as inseparable as the intertwining rivers that flow through the heart of the Black Country. Their childhood memories were embedded in the cobbled streets of Walsall, a town echoing with a melodic fusion of history and modernity. Each brick, every alleyway, seemed to hum with whispered tales, painting the canvas of their existence with enigmatic strokes.

One peculiar night, under a sky painted with strokes of midnight blue, illuminated by the ethereal dance of the silvery moon and the distant stars, Suzanne and Cheryl found themselves amidst the silent reverie of Walsall's old town centre.

The clock tower, a silent sentinel of time, stood amidst the winding streets echoing tales of times long past. Each tick of its ancient hands seemed to reverberate with whispered secrets, untold tales echoing amidst the silent night.

As they walked, the gentle rustle of the autumn leaves beneath their feet played in harmony with the soft, haunting whispers of the wind. It was a night where the boundary between the earthly and ethereal seemed as fragile as the silken threads of a spider's web glistening in the moonlight.

It was Cheryl who first sensed the presence. A cold, ethereal touch, as if the winds themselves bore the silent imprints of souls long departed. Amidst the haunting silence, where the echoes of their footsteps danced with the muted whispers of the winds, a shadow emerged.

It was neither formless nor distinct, a spectral entity echoing a haunting dance of light and darkness. The old town centre, with its ancient edifices and silent streets, bore witness to the emergence of the Walsall Wraith.

The Wraith, a figure clad in the garbs of an era long past, haunted the silent pathways, a spectral entity seeking justice for a crime veiled in the silent annals of history. Each echo of its haunting footsteps resonated with the silent cries of injustice, echoing amidst the ancient bricks and mortar of the old town.

Suzanne, a soul touched by the subtle sensitivities of the world unseen, felt a profound connection to the spectral entity. Each echo of its haunting footsteps, each silent cry, resonated within the depths of her soul.

Cheryl, though rooted in the tangible, could not escape the eerie, haunting allure of the Wraith. Amidst the cold, silken threads of the haunting winds, they followed the spectral entity, silent witnesses to a tale unfolding from the depths of the silent past.

The Wraith led them through the winding pathways of the old town, each street, every alleyway echoing with the haunting cries of justice unserved. The ancient clock tower, its hands frozen in time, bore silent witness to the eerie dance of the spectral entity.

Amidst the haunting silence of the old town, beneath the eerie luminescence of the moonlit night, Suzanne and Cheryl stood amidst a spectacle that transcended the corporeal existence.

The Wraith, though silent, echoed a tale of betrayal, of a crime buried within the silent annals of time. Its haunting cries, echoing amidst the silent night, sought redemption, a justice that lay buried amidst the silent bricks and echoing pathways of Walsall.

As the first rays of dawn kissed the silent edifice of the old town, the Wraith, its spectral dance echoing the haunting cries of the silent past, dissolved into the ethereal embrace of the emerging light.

Suzanne and Cheryl, forever changed, ventured back into the world of the living, the eerie dance of the Wraith and its silent cries for justice imprinted within their souls.

The old town centre, with its ancient bricks and silent pathways, bore the imprints of souls and tales that transcended the earthly existence. Suzanne and Cheryl, though silent, bore the haunting echoes of the Walsall Wraith within their souls.

In the silent nights, when the eerie dance of the silvery moon cast haunting reflections upon the silent streets of Walsall, the whispers of the Wraith could be heard, echoing amidst the winding pathways, a spectral entity seeking justice for a crime veiled in the haunting echoes of time.

The town, though modern, bore the silent imprints of the past. And Suzanne and Cheryl, though rooted in the tangible, were forever touched by the eerie, haunting allure of the Walsall Wraith - a spectral dance of light and darkness, justice and betrayal, echoing amidst the silent, moonlit nights of the Black Country.

OLDBURY'S OLD INN PATRONS

Dianne and Tracy had always been drawn to the rustic charm of Oldbury. The cobbled streets and archaic architecture told tales of an era where every brick and pathway was imbued with history, a narrative tapestry spun from centuries of existence. Amidst these winding lanes, nestled quietly in the shadows of time, was the Old Inn - a place as enigmatic as the tales that whispered through its ancient walls.

The Old Inn was not just a pub; it was a relic of the past, a silent spectator to the ceaseless dance of time. The timeworn wooden panels, the crackling fireplace, the echo of laughter, and clinks of glasses carried the resonance of generations.

Dianne and Tracy, two friends with an insatiable appetite for the enigmatic, would often find themselves nestled in a quiet corner of the Old Inn. Their laughter and stories would merge with the ambient symphony of voices, an everlasting tune that swirled around the old, dimly lit rooms.

One fateful evening, as rain danced against the windows and wind whispered enigmatic sonnets, they found themselves alone in the enchanting solitude of the pub. The clock, as old as the inn itself, chimed eerily in the distance. Time seemed suspended in a perpetual dance, swirling amidst the haunting melodies that echoed through the pub's silent chambers.

They were not alone. The air was thick with an unspeakable presence, an ethereal entity that lurked in the profound depths of the shadows. A cold gust of wind, inexplicable and haunting, curled around the friends, sending shivers down their spines and extinguishing the roaring flames of the fireplace.

In the dim, flickering light of the lanterns, silhouettes and shadows danced an eerie waltz. The resonance of footsteps, hauntingly familiar yet profoundly unnerving, echoed amidst the silent walls of the inn.

It was in this haunting solitude that Dianne and Tracy encountered the ethereal occupants of the Old Inn. A shadowy figure, an enigmatic silhouette cloaked in the robes of history, emerged from the silent darkness. His eyes, voids of eternal depths, pierced through the unsettling silence with a haunting gaze.

Tracy, her breath suspended in the profound silence, felt the touch of icy fingers curling around her soul. Dianne, paralyzed by the haunting gaze of the spectral entity, stood amidst the silent dance of time and eternity.

They were silent witnesses to a narrative as ancient as the inn itself. The figure, a silent spectre of a bygone era, told tales of betrayal, love, and unspeakable tragedies. The silent walls of the Old Inn bore witness to the spectral dance of figures, ghostly entities echoing haunting sonnets of unspeakable sorrows and eternal lament.

As the clock chimed the haunting melodies of midnight, the inn resonated with the eerie echoes of ghostly wails. The wooden panels, the silent rooms, the extinguished fireplace - every corner of the inn was imbued with the haunting presence of souls trapped in perpetual dance of sorrow and tragedy.

Dianne and Tracy, enveloped in the icy embrace of the spectral entities, witnessed the unfolding of a tragic tale. A narrative of love betrayed, of lives extinguished amidst the silent spectres of deceit and betrayal.

As dawn kissed the silent horizons, casting the first rays of light amidst the enigmatic shadows of the inn, the spectral figures dissolved into the ethereal embrace of light. The haunting echoes, the icy fingers, the unspeakable sorrows - every spectral entity retreated into the silent depths of the inn's ancient walls.

Dianne and Tracy, forever changed, emerged from the haunted embrace of the Old Inn. The silent streets of Oldbury, echoing the haunting melodies of history and time, bore witness to souls touched by the enigmatic dance of the spectral.

The Old Inn, as ancient as the cobblestone paths that wound through the heart of Oldbury, harboured unspeakable secrets. Every night, as the clock chimed the haunting sonnets of midnight, the inn came alive with the eerie dance of spectral entities.

Haunted by the silent echoes of tragic tales and unspeakable sorrows, the inn stood as a silent relic of a bygone era. Dianne and Tracy, their souls forever touched by the enigmatic dance of the spectral, bore the haunting echoes of Oldbury's Old Inn within the profound depths of their existence.

In the silent nights, where moonlight danced amidst the ancient pathways of Oldbury, the haunting echoes of ghostly wails, of unspeakable tragedies, whispered the enigmatic sonnets of the Old Inn - a place where history, tragedy, and the spectral danced in perpetual unison.

THE CHAINMAKER'S CHANT

Carry had always been fond of old towns and the history that wrapped them like an old, enigmatic, and comforting shawl. The echoes of the past, reverberating through time, casting long, ominous, yet somehow inviting shadows that lured the curious and the brave alike. Cradley Heath was such a town; its darkened alleyways and aged structures breathed an amalgamation of stories each night, resurrecting phantoms of a time long lost, yet never truly forgotten.

Steven, Carry's older brother, was more pragmatic, a man of tangible proofs, yet he too couldn't deny the eerie charm that emanated from the dilapidated buildings and the cold, cobblestone paths. Their walks together, amidst the twilight hours, were silent testimonies to the dance of this dual existence – of the logical and the ethereal.

One crisp autumn evening, they found themselves wandering close to an old, abandoned workshop, once famous for its chains, a symbol of the industrial vigour of a century past. The 'Bates Chain Making', as the faded signboard announced, was now but a whisper of its former self, its doors locked, its soul ostensibly silent but for the unseen echoes that hummed, haunting the peripheries of hearing.

Carry, drawn inexplicably, approached the old building. Steven, ever the protector, followed, his sceptical eyes scanning the surroundings, feet crunching on the gravel that seemed to moan under his weight.

The moon, a silent spectre, cast an eerie glow that night, illuminating the outline of the workshop in a spectral dance of light and shadows. As they stood before it, a strange clanking noise resonated through the silence, piercing the night with its ominous notes.

Carry's heart quickened. She turned towards Steven, whose eyes were now wide, reflecting the silvery touch of the moon, and something else - a fear that dared not speak its name. The clanking continued, rhythmical, foreboding, echoing the mournful chants of an era where chains were forged amidst flames and sweat.

Yet, there was something else, a melodic, haunting tune that seemed to breathe life into the night, its eerie notes painting the cold air with spectral fingers, drawing the siblings closer, luring them into a dance they hadn't rehearsed for.

The doors of the workshop, though rusted and ostensibly locked, gave way with a gentle push. Carry and Steven stepped into an era untouched by the hands of time. Amidst the rusted tools and darkened corners, the clanking grew louder, a rhythmic, haunting symphony of metal against metal.

There, amidst the shadows and the ghostly illumination of the moon, spectres of chainmakers past danced to the eternal rhythm of their craft. These apparitions, worn and ethereal, eyes imbued with the flames of a time long lost yet never forgotten, forged chains with hands that told tales of sorrow, of vigour, of an undying spirit that defied the clutches of time.

Carry, caught in the ethereal ballet, watched, as spectral hands, glowing with the touch of another world, danced amidst the flames. Steven, pragmatic no more, stood, a silent witness to the communion of eras, of lives lost and remembered.

The ghostly chant of the chainmakers hummed a melancholic yet somehow comforting tune. A narrative of lives spent amidst the clatter of chains, of spirits bound yet free, of a craft that defied the silence of the grave, echoing through time in haunting, yet beautiful notes of existence.

As dawn kissed the edges of the night, dissipating the spectral dance of light and shadows, Carry and Steven, forever changed, stepped out of the 'Bates Chain Making' workshop. The clanking ceased, yet its echoes remained, a haunting lullaby that would dance in the silent nights of Cradley Heath, an unutterable testimony to the existence that stretched beyond the palpable, echoing the undying song of the chainmakers.

The siblings never spoke of that night, yet in the silence of their knowing glances, amidst the quiet nights when the moon danced in its silvery splendour, they heard it - the unutterable chant of the chainmakers, a haunting, beautiful symphony of an era, of souls, that refused to be forgotten.

The town of Cradley Heath, silent yet echoing with the unsung ballads of time, bore witness to the eternal dance of the chainmakers. A dance of spirits that defied the clutches of time, painting the silence of the night with the haunting, yet beautiful chants of existence eternal. In this silent testimony of eras past and present, Carry and Steven found an unutterable connection, an eerie yet comforting dance amidst the silence and the chants, a dance of the living, and the spectral chainmakers of Cradley Heath.

BRIERLEY HILL'S
HAUNTING HYMN

Tony had always found a peculiar solace in the silent nights of Brierley Hill. In the stillness, the old town whispered secrets of bygone days, and the winds carried haunting, yet harmonic, melodies of a time forgotten. Richard, his childhood friend, shared this peculiar affection. Though the hands of time had drawn lines upon their faces and the vigour of youth had given way to the solemnity of age, the bond forged amidst the mystical silences of the old town remained unyielding.

On an eve where the full moon painted silvery streaks upon the landscape, and the stars whispered the ancient tales of cosmic ballets, the duo found themselves wandering the familiar paths of their cherished town.

Their feet, guided by the unseen hands of fate, led them to an old chapel, long abandoned, yet still pulsating with the spiritual energies of a time when it teemed with life. The Gothic architecture, with spires that seemed to pierce the heavens, stood as a solemn testimony to an era where voices raised in holy harmonies sought communion with the divine.

This chapel held special memories for Tony and Richard. In their youthful days, they had been part of the choir, their young voices contributing to the divine symphonies that ascended the celestial realms. But time, the eternal river, had flowed incessantly, and the chapel had fallen into silence, the divine hymns giving way to an eerie, yet profound quietude.

As they stood before the sacred relic of their past, an inexplicable phenomenon stirred the silent night. The doors of the chapel, rusted and untouched for decades, creaked open, as if beckoning the old friends into the sanctified realms of their youthful days.

Tony and Richard, entranced by the enigmatic call, stepped into a world where the boundaries of time dissolved, and the celestial echoed the hymns of angels and men in eternal unison.

The chapel, though desolate and worn, radiated a divine glow. The sacred altars, though covered in the dust of ages, shimmered with a heavenly aura. In this divine twilight, the souls of the departed, those who once raised their voices in holy symphony, returned to the silent abode of their earthly sojourn.

The air vibrated with the haunting, yet divine notes of 'Ave Maria'. Each note, profound and holy, reverberated with the celestial energies of angels and saints in divine communion. Tony and Richard, standing amidst the haunting harmonies, felt their souls uplifted, the temporal giving way to the eternal, the earthly dissolving into the celestial.

The stained-glass windows, though aged and brittle, painted portraits of divine narratives in silvery hues. The Holy Mother, saints, and angels looked upon the mortal guests with eyes radiating the infinite compassion and solemnity of the heavens.

Every corner of the chapel, every sacred artefact, every divine image, vibrated with the haunting echoes of the celestial hymn. Tony and Richard, their souls stripped of the temporal garments, stood amidst the divine dance of heavenly entities.

As the haunting melody of 'Ave Maria' reached its celestial crescendo, a profound silence, sacred and eerie, descended upon the chapel. The divine entities, the sacred harmonies, the holy vibrations, retreated into the mystical realms of the eternal.

Tony and Richard, marked by the divine touch, emerged from the chapel into the silent night of Brierley Hill. The old town, with its ancient paths and mystical energies, stood as a silent witness to the divine communion that transcended the boundaries of time and existence.

No words were spoken, no testimonies given. The haunting hymn of the old chapel remained a sacred secret, a divine narrative, echoing in the silent nights of Brierley Hill, when the moon painted silvery portraits and the stars whispered the ancient tales of cosmic ballets.

The old chapel, silent yet echoing with the haunting hymn of 'Ave Maria', stood as a portal where the temporal and the eternal, the earthly and the celestial, danced in unison – a dance witnessed by the silent stars, the mystical moon, and two souls forever marked by the divine touch of Brierley Hill's haunting hymn.

THE SEDGLEY SEER

David, an average man with a commonplace job in the industrial town of Sedgley, had a life as grey and unmarked as the concrete buildings that boxed in the horizon. He was never the one to attract attention, his existence hummed quietly in the rhythm of the everyday life. But as the years rolled on, a profound change overcame him. It was subtle at first, almost imperceptible, like the first hint of dawn quietly dispelling the darkness of the night.

It began with an eerie sense of déjà vu, occurrences too uncanny to dismiss as mere coincidences. A foreboding chill would settle in his bones, casting dark, ominous shadows of events yet to pass. He'd envision accidents before they occurred, sense the rain before the skies would even cloud, and hear whispered secrets that would later prove true. These spectral premonitions filled David with an unspeakable dread.

One cold, silent night, a sinister vision came to him, more vivid and terrifying than any before. A shadowy figure of a child, her piercing cries echoing in the chilling wind, appeared before David. The unsettling spectre would weave in and out of his nightly torments, turning his slumbers into a haunted playfield of ghostly visitations.

As the days turned to weeks, and weeks into haunting months, David's quiet life unravelled into a sinister symphony of ghastly premonitions. The boundaries between the waking world and eerie spectres became indistinguishable. Every corner he turned, every street he walked, whispered the haunting lullabies of unseen entities.

During one of his tormenting visions, a particularly insidious premonition gripped him. He saw the old chapel at the edge of the town, long abandoned, yet echoing the sinister chants of a ghostly congregation. In this vision, amidst the pews covered with the dust of decades and beneath the silent gaze of the stained glass, stood the shadowy figure of the weeping child.

Every cell in David's body urged him to escape, yet an insidious force drew him towards the ghostly echoes of the chapel. One fateful night, under the sinister glow of the moon, he found himself standing before the crumbling edifice.

Inside, the eerie silence was pregnant with unspeakable secrets. A sudden gust of wind blew open the doors and David, compelled by a force beyond comprehension, stepped inside. Every echo of his footsteps resonated with the haunting cries of souls long departed.

It was there, amidst the sacred decay, that the ghastly spectre of the child, pale and forlorn, revealed the tragic tale of her untimely demise. David, trapped in the spectral dance of his haunting visions and the child's unspeakable narrative, became the unwilling bearer of Sedgley's sinister secrets.

The townsfolk, once indifferent to the unassuming David, now cast him wary glances. Whispers of the haunted chapel and David's eerie premonitions slithered through the town like sinister tendrils.

As technology painted every moment, capturing life in the unyielding glare of social media's gaze, David's haunting ordeal remained shrouded in a sinister mystery. No digital footprint bore witness to the eerie spectre, and no electronic device could capture the ghostly cries that echoed in the haunted chambers of David's soul.

The modern world, vibrant and pulsating with the unyielding march of technology, bore silent witness to an ancient, sinister dance; where the spectral cries of a child long departed, and the eerie premonitions of a man too ordinary to be noticed, wove an unspeakable narrative.

A narrative that whispered the haunting lullabies of spectral entities, painting the grey, concrete existence of Sedgley with the sinister hues of unspeakable secrets and eerie echoes, forever lost in the silent corridors of the unseen.

THE WATCHER OF
WARLEY WOODS

It was a cold evening in the heart of November when Peter first heard of the woods. Warley Woods, as they were known to the inhabitants of the Black Country, stood enigmatic, with trees that rose like sentinels, their limbs stretching out as if reaching for something in the eerie silence of the night.

His son, Dylan, was a curious soul. The eight-year-old had the kind of imagination that turned every corner into a realm of wonder, every shadow into a mysterious ally, and every light into a guide to enchanted lands.

One evening, as the twilight draped its ethereal cloak around the world, transforming the ordinary into the mystical, Dylan came running to Peter, his eyes wide with a mix of terror and exhilaration.

"Daddy, I saw him! The watcher of the woods," he exclaimed, his little chest heaving with each breath.

Peter knelt down to Dylan's level, his eyes soft yet curious. "Saw who, son?" he asked gently, brushing his son's tousled hair.

"The old man, Daddy. He stands by the big oak tree, with the green eyes that glow in the dark. He watches us play," Dylan's voice trembled, a mix of the cold and the remnant of fear, tinged with a bizarre sense of safety.

Peter had heard the stories, every local had. Warley Woods was said to be haunted by a spirit, neither malicious nor benign, but a silent watcher. A protector, some claimed, especially attentive to children who ventured into the woods.

Days turned into weeks, the chills of November giving way to the frost of December. Dylan and his friends continued their escapades into the woods, and with each venture, stories of the Watcher grew more vivid. Each child had their own account, but common to all was the depiction of an old man, with deep-set green eyes, standing sentinel by the grand old oak tree.

The parents, including Peter, listened to these stories with a mix of amusement and unease. The woods had always been a place of mystery. Generations had grown up with tales of the Watcher. None could say when these stories began or from whence the Watcher came, but his enigmatic presence was as integral to Warley Woods as the ancient trees themselves.

One frosty evening, as the skies painted a gloomy picture, echoing the silent dread that often accompanies long, dark nights, Dylan ventured into the woods, alone. The allure of a freshly fallen snow, casting an ethereal glow, proving too irresistible.

As the shadows of the night danced ominously around him, Dylan felt an unsettling presence. The woods, usually a place of wonder and excitement, now exuded an aura of haunting solitude. The silence was punctuated by the crunch of his boots on the snowy pathway.

It was then that he saw him - the Watcher. An old man, his features barely visible, yet eyes of green that gleamed in the dark, echoing an otherworldly presence.

Frozen with both fear and fascination, Dylan stood motionless. The Watcher, silent and enigmatic, stared at the boy. In those eternal moments of silent communion, a strange warmth enveloped Dylan. The haunting cold, the eerie silence, the menacing dark - all dissolved into an unspeakable comfort.

Peter, realising the absence of his son, ventured frantically into the woods. The haunting tales of the Watcher, once distant echoes of local lore, now churned menacingly in his mind. He found Dylan by the old oak tree, unharmed, the enigmatic green eyes of the Watcher looming over him - neither menacing nor benign, just watching, guarding.

The incident left an indelible mark on the town of Warley. The children continued to play in the woods, their laughter echoing the silent, enigmatic watchfulness of the spectral guardian. The parents, including Peter, were left to grapple with the enigma. A ghost story that was neither haunting nor comforting. A spectral presence that neither menaced nor protected. It just was, silent and enigmatic.

In the heart of Warley Woods, beneath the silent gaze of the ancient trees and the eerie echoes of the unknown, the tale of the Watcher weaved itself into the fabric of the town. Neither entirely believed nor entirely dismissed.

The Black Country, with its rich industrial past and haunting landscapes, bore silent witness to the spectral dance of the living and the dead. In the eerie silence of Warley Woods, amidst the shadows of the ancient trees and the enigmatic gaze of the Watcher, the boundaries between this world and the next blurred into an unspeakable enigma. A tale as haunting as it was silent, echoing the eerie dance of the unknown amidst the silent trees of the enigmatic woods.

THE GORNAL GHOST LIGHT

The village of Gornal was a place of silence, where the old and new coexisted in a delicate dance of quietude. Nestled amidst the brooding landscapes of the Black Country, time seemed to have suspended its relentless march. Here, stories of the past wove seamlessly into the fabric of the present, echoing the ancient whispers of forgotten souls. On silent nights, when the moon shone with an ethereal glow, casting long, haunting shadows through narrow lanes and cobblestone pathways, the village seemed to hold its breath, ensnared in an enchanting spell.

Harry was born amidst this enigmatic silence. A child of Gornal, the village's haunting serenity echoed in his quiet disposition. He was familiar with every ancient tree, every whispering breeze, and every mystical legend that danced in the silence of the haunting woods surrounding the village. Yet, among the myriad tales that hung in the air, none was as compelling and ominous as that of the Gornal Ghost Light.

It was said that on nights when silence reigned supreme, a ghostly lantern light would wander the village, its eerie glow casting ominous illuminations upon the ancient stones. Held by no hand, guided by no human presence, the light moved with an enigmatic grace, echoing a haunting melody of unspeakable dread and enigmatic allure.

Harry had heard the stories from old Mrs. Atkins, who claimed the light was the soul of a lost wanderer forever condemned to haunt the village. Young Emma swore it was a mystical entity, a guardian of ancient secrets buried deep within the heart of Gornal. Each villager, young and old, held a tale, whispered in the haunting silence of enigmatic nights.

One silent night, as the moon bathed Gornal in its silken glow, Harry found himself drawn into the enigmatic dance of silence and shadow. The village, ensnared in the spectral embrace of moonlight, echoed the haunting whispers of forgotten souls. It was on this night, amidst the eerie quietude, that Harry encountered the Gornal Ghost Light.

The light emerged from the depths of the woods, its ghostly illumination casting an eerie glow upon the ancient trees. Harry, ensnared by an unspeakable dread yet compelled by an enigmatic allure, followed the light's haunting dance. The village, bathed in an ominous glow, revealed its hidden secrets in the eerie illuminations of the ghost light.

As Harry wandered the silent lanes, the light led him to the old church, its ancient stones echoing the silent prayers of forgotten souls. The church, abandoned and silent, stood as a spectral testament to a time long past. Here, amidst the haunting silence, the ghost light revealed its enigmatic secret.

Inside the church, illuminated by the eerie glow, lay the tomb of Sir Reginald Allerton, a nobleman of ancient times, whose tragic demise was shrouded in mystery. The villagers spoke of Sir Reginald in hushed tones; his tale was one of love, betrayal, and unspeakable dread.

It was said that Sir Reginald was betrayed by his closest confidante, and in the haunting silence of a moonlit night, he met his untimely end. The Gornal Ghost Light, as the villagers whispered, was Sir Reginald's soul, forever condemned to wander the village, echoing the silent lament of betrayal and loss.

Harry, standing amidst the eerie silence, felt the cold touch of the spectral light. The ancient tomb, echoing the silent sobs of a betrayed soul, unveiled the unspeakable – the haunting presence of Sir Reginald, his eyes echoing the dread of betrayal, his hands reaching out from the depths of time.

The silence of the night was pierced by the ghostly echoes of a haunting lament, a melody of love and loss, betrayal and dread. Harry, ensnared in the spectral embrace of the ghost light, witnessed the dance of the betrayed soul, forever condemned to echo the silent melody of unspeakable sorrow.

As dawn broke, casting its golden hue upon the haunting silence of the night's eerie dance, Harry, forever changed, carried the silent echoes of the Gornal Ghost Light. The village, awakening to the gentle embrace of dawn, remained ensnared in the enigmatic dance of silence and shadow.

For amidst the serene landscapes of Gornal, where ancient trees whispered the tales of forgotten souls, the ghost light danced its silent, haunting melody, a spectral echo of love, loss, and the unspeakable dread of betrayal forever imprinted upon the silent stones of the enigmatic village.

WHISPERS OF WILLENHALL

Duncan had always held a fascination for the old Willenhall lanes, where the rich history of the town whispered through the brick walls of the ancient structures. Each building, each cobblestone seemed impregnated with tales of yore, echoing the lives of those who had once walked these paths.

As a child, Duncan often wandered the lanes, his ears tuned to the mysterious sounds that sometimes filled the air. Whispers, they were; delicate and ephemeral, yet charged with a potent energy, a silent testament to an era long past yet alive in the silent air of Willenhall.

Among all the relics of the past, none was more enchanting to Duncan than the old locksmith shops, remnants of a time when Willenhall was known as the town of locks and keys. It was said that the skill of Willenhall's locksmiths was unmatchable, their creations not just locks but intricate pieces of art that safeguarded the town's most precious secrets.

One locksmith shop, in particular, held Duncan's attention. Abandoned, with its doors locked for decades, it sat silent and brooding amidst the thriving life of the modern town. No one remembered its origins or the hands that had once turned its keys. Yet it stood, an eternal enigma, its silence echoing the whispers of unspeakable mysteries.

One moonlit night, as the silvery beams danced upon the silent lanes of Willenhall, Duncan found himself drawn towards the old locksmith shop. The town slept in the haunting embrace of the night, yet the locksmith shop, bathed in the eerie glow of the moon, echoed the silent whispers of the locksmiths of old.

The door, locked for decades, yielded under Duncan's touch, opening into a world where time stood still. The air was dense with the silent echoes of the past, each lock, each key a silent witness to the lives that had once turned them. As Duncan wandered amidst the relics of yore, the whispers grew louder, echoing the silent dance of the locksmiths of old.

There, amidst the haunting silence, Duncan witnessed the ethereal ballet of ghostly figures, their hands weaving the ancient dance of lock and key. Each movement, each whisper echoing the secrets of a craft perfected over lifetimes. The air was thick with the potent energy of creation, each lock, each key a masterpiece born from the silent dance of spectral hands.

As Duncan stood, mesmerised, the ghostly locksmiths, in their ethereal ballet, unveiled the secrets of their craft. Each whisper, each movement a silent sonnet of skill and artistry. The locks, intricate and complex, seemed imbued with a mystical energy, each turn of the key opening not just doors but gateways to unspeakable mysteries.

The moon, in its silken dance, cast ghostly illuminations upon the spectral ballet, its silvery beams echoing the haunting melody of the whispers of old. Duncan, ensnared in the enigmatic dance, bore witness to the silent birth of masterpieces, each lock, each key an eternal testament to the skill of Willenhall's locksmiths of yore.

As dawn kissed the night, weaving its golden hues amidst the silvery beams of the moon, the ghostly locksmiths, their spectral ballet complete, faded into the silent air of the ancient shop. Duncan, forever changed, carried within him the silent echoes of the whispers of old.

The town of Willenhall, awakening to the embrace of the dawn, remained oblivious to the mystical dance that had unfolded amidst the silent lanes. Yet, each lock, each key that adorned the ancient doors, echoed the silent sonnets of the locksmiths of old, their skill, their artistry forever engraved in the silent stones of the enigmatic town.

Duncan, his soul echoing the whispers of the past, wandered the lanes of Willenhall, each turn of a key a haunting reminder of the spectral ballet of the locksmiths of old. For amidst the silence of the ancient town, the ghostly whispers of skill and mystery danced in the wind, a silent sonnet of a craft, an artistry, a legacy born from the enigmatic dance of Willenhall's locksmiths of yore.

THE BLACKHEATH BANSHEE

The brisk autumn air in Blackheath carried a chill that seemed to cut through even the warmest of coats. As the leaves turned from green to brilliant hues of red and gold, the town, with its quiet streets and ageing architecture, bore witness to the silent passing of another year.

Yet for Henry, a lifelong resident of the town, the beauty of autumn was marred by a haunting echo of the past—a mournful wail that resonated through the silent nights of Blackheath, a harrowing reminder of a tragedy buried deep within the annals of the town's mining history.

As the townsfolk slept, nestled within the quiet embrace of their homes, Henry alone was a captive audience to the sorrowful wails of the Blackheath Banshee. Each note, potent with anguish, reverberated through the silent streets, echoing a tale of loss and despair.

Blackheath, with its rich mining heritage, bore the scars of an industry that had once flourished amidst the depths of the earth. The mines, now silent and abandoned, were haunting monuments to a time when men, clad in dust and grime, ventured deep within the earth, their lives tethered to the precious coal that lay buried within its silent embrace.

On one fateful day, as the autumn air danced with the first whispers of winter, tragedy struck the town of Blackheath. The mines, silent witnesses to the aspirations and fears of the miners who toiled within their depths, became the eternal resting place for souls trapped amidst the stone and earth.

Henry, a young lad then, bore witness to the haunting aftermath

—a town gripped by loss, families shattered, and a silence that echoed the unspeakable tragedy. As the mines closed, their silent halls entombing the souls of the lost, the town of Blackheath was forever marked by an unspoken sorrow.

The wail of the Banshee, potent and harrowing, was a silent sonnet of the anguish that permeated the air of Blackheath. Each autumn, as the air turned crisp, and the leaves whispered the silent passage of time, the Banshee's wail echoed through the silent nights—a haunting reminder of the tragedy that lay buried within the silent mines.

Henry, his soul scarred by the haunting echoes of the past, wandered the silent streets of Blackheath. Each wail, each note, a potent reminder of the lives lost, the dreams shattered, and the silence that bore witness to the unutterable grief.

The town, oblivious to the haunting serenade that marked the silent nights of autumn, slept in quiet repose. Yet, Henry, ensnared by the spectral echoes of the Banshee's wail, bore solitary witness to the haunting symphony of anguish and loss.

The Banshee, a spectral entity cloaked in sorrow, wandered the silent mines of Blackheath. Her wails, echoing the silent tragedy of lives lost and dreams unfulfilled, were a haunting sonnet of a town marked by the unutterable silence of grief.

As another autumn descended upon Blackheath, the Banshee's wails echoed through the silent nights—a spectral sonnet that bore witness to the silent tragedy enshrined within the town's mining past. The silent streets, the ageing architecture, the whispering leaves—all silent witnesses to the haunting melody of sorrow that permeated the air.

Henry, a solitary figure amidst the silent embrace of autumn, bore the scars of a tragedy unspoken. The wails of the Banshee, potent and haunting, echoed the silent symphony of loss and grief—a town marked by the unutterable silence of a tragedy buried deep within the annals of its mining history.

As the leaves turned, and another year passed into the silent embrace of time, the town of Blackheath, with its quiet streets and haunting past, remained ensnared by the spectral echoes of the Banshee's wail—a haunting reminder of the silence that bore witness to the unutterable grief of lives lost amidst the silent embrace of the earth.

KINGSWINFORD'S KITCHEN SPIRIT

Debbie had always been fascinated by the grandeur of the old Victorian home that sat abandoned at the end of her street in Kingswinford. The house, with its intricately carved wooden frames and ivy-clad exterior, emanated an enigmatic allure that beckoned the curious souls who dared venture close to its forbidden embrace. Even amidst the pervading silence, stories of mysterious happenings swirled in hushed tones, adding to the mansion's enigmatic allure.

One evening, as the tenebrous embrace of night shrouded the town and the moon unveiled its silver hue, Debbie found herself inexplicably drawn to the house. A cacophony of nocturnal sounds permeated the silence, and the whispers of trees swaying to the gentle caress of the wind narrated untold stories of the mansion's haunting past.

As Debbie stepped closer, an olfactory tapestry of scents wafted through the cold night air. The aroma of baking bread, the spiced scent of an old-fashioned stew - the intricate dance of olfactory notes painted a spectral scene of a kitchen once bustling with life.

Debbie stood there, amidst the silence of the night, the haunting aroma enveloping her, painting vivid scenes of a time long past. The mansion, though known to be abandoned for decades, in that moment, seemed to echo the spectral rhythms of a family once nestled within its grandeur.

The windows, veiled in an eerie silence, reflected the haunting dance of the moon's silver rays, unveiling spectral scenes of an old woman, her hands, weathered with the silent passage of time, engaged in the eternal dance of creation amidst the kitchen's silent embrace.

Debbie, ensnared by the haunting spectacle, bore witness to a spectral ballet - the clattering of utensils, the silent sizzling of an ethereal stew, the soft hum of a melody echoing the silent rhythms of a time long past.

Kingswinford, a town imbued with tales of the mysterious and the unexplainable, bore the silent echoes of a history steeped in enigma. Yet the grandeur of the old Victorian mansion, with its haunting allure, remained an unsolved mystery.

Days turned into weeks, and weeks into months, yet the haunting aroma that pervaded the silent nights remained an enigmatic sonnet, echoing the spectral dance of a time steeped in silence.

Debbie, marked by the haunting experience, would often find herself drawn to the enigmatic embrace of the mansion. Each visit, under the silent gaze of the moon, unveiled ethereal scenes of a family - spectral figures engaged in the silent dance of life amidst the mansion's haunting grandeur.

The town of Kingswinford, though veiled in the silent embrace of the mundane, was home to mysteries that defied explanation. The old Victorian mansion, with its haunting presence, remained a spectral entity - echoing the untold stories of a family ensnared within its silent walls.

The aroma of cooking, the clattering of utensils, the haunting hum of a melody echoing the silent passage of time - these remained enigmatic sonnets painting vivid scenes of a life once nestled within the mansion's grandeur.

As years turned into decades, and the silent passage of time marked the town's evolving landscape, the mansion, though abandoned, remained imbued with an enigmatic allure.

Debbie, now marked by the silent echoes of the past, would often recount the haunting experience to those willing to venture close to the enigmatic embrace of the mansion. The spectral aroma, the ethereal sounds - these remained haunting echoes of a time long past, yet vividly alive within the silent walls of the grand Victorian home.

The Kingswinford's Kitchen Spirit, as it came to be known, remained an enigmatic entity - a haunting dance of olfactory notes and spectral sounds that defied the silent passage of time. Amidst the grandeur of the mansion, the silent echo of a family once nestled within its embrace, remained a haunting melody - echoing the untold stories of a time steeped in enigma and the unexplainable.

THE PRINCELY
PHANTOM OF PENN

Kelly had always been fascinated by the majesty of Penn Wood. She was born and raised in the heart of the Black Country, and Penn, with its sprawling acres of ancient trees and mystical atmosphere, was her sanctuary. It was a world apart from the buzz of industry and modern life, a place where time seemed to stand still, and the whispers of the past could be heard in the rustling of the leaves.

One evening, as the amber hues of the setting sun painted a golden silhouette against the backdrop of the ancient forest, Kelly ventured deeper into Penn Wood. The tranquillity was ethereal, the sounds of the woods harmonising with the silent whisper of the evening breeze.

It was in the haunting embrace of this silence that Kelly first heard the whispers - soft, enigmatic murmurs that seemed to echo the untold stories of a time long past. She followed the haunting lilt of these whispers deeper into the woods, where the golden hues of the setting sun unveiled the spectral figure of a nobleman - his gaze, eternal, overlooking the vast expanse of his lands.

The nobleman, adorned in attire befitting of his stature, stood amidst the haunting embrace of the woods - a spectral entity echoing the silent rhythms of an era when Penn Wood bore witness to the grandeur of his reign.

Kelly, ensnared by the ethereal presence, bore witness to the Princely Phantom of Penn - a figure cloaked in enigma, his silent gaze reflecting the untold stories of a time when his word was law, and the vast acres of Penn Wood, his kingdom.

Each evening, as the amber hues of the setting sun painted ethereal silhouettes against the backdrop of the ancient woods, Kelly would return - each visit unveiling haunting echoes of a time steeped in majesty and grandeur.

The Princely Phantom of Penn was no mere spectre. He was a testament to an era when the woods were alive with the silent footsteps of nobility - a time when the rustling leaves bore witness to the grandeur of a nobleman whose presence marked the landscape of Penn.

The town, though steeped in the silent embrace of modernity, bore the silent echoes of a past that refused to be forgotten. Each generation, marked by the enigmatic allure of Penn Wood, would recount haunting tales of the Princely Phantom - a spectral entity, forever ensnared within the silent embrace of his kingdom.

Kelly, now marked by the haunting encounters, was not one for superstitions. Yet, each evening, as the silent whisper of the woods called out to her, she would venture deep into the embrace of Penn - each visit unveiling ethereal scenes of a nobleman, his silent gaze forever overseeing the vast expanse of his lands.

The woods, though alive with the silent rhythms of nature, bore the spectral echo of a time long past. Each tree, each leaf, each silent whisper of the evening breeze, painted haunting scenes of an era when the Princely Phantom of Penn reigned supreme.

Kelly, though a child of modernity, was now a silent witness to a haunting dance of the past and present. The enigmatic allure of the woods, marked by the silent gaze of a nobleman, unveiled the untold stories of a time when majesty and grandeur marked the landscape of Penn.

As years turned into decades, and the silent passage of time weaved its enigmatic sonnet, Kelly, now marked by the haunting echoes of the woods, became the silent custodian of its enigmatic allure. Each generation, ensnared by the haunting embrace of Penn Wood, would bear witness to the Princely Phantom - a spectral entity echoing the untold stories of a time when majesty, grandeur, and the silent whisper of the woods, marked the eternal dance of Penn's enigmatic embrace.

The Black Country, though marked by the silent rhythms of industry and modernity, bore the silent echo of a haunting past. Penn Wood, with its enigmatic allure, remained a haunting testament to a time when the silent whisper of the woods unveiled the spectral dance of a nobleman - forever overseeing the vast expanse of his kingdom, eternally ensnared within the haunting embrace of his silent, majestic woods.

DARLASTON'S DANCING SHADOWS

Darlaston, a quiet town nestled deep within the heart of the Black Country, bore witness to an eerie phenomenon that haunted its streets long after the clock had struck midnight. The locals spoke of it only in hushed whispers, for they knew the tale was far from mere superstition; it was a bone-chilling truth that could send shivers down even the bravest spine.

Barry, a man whose scepticism knew no bounds, had heard the chilling tales circulating through Darlaston's close-knit community. He dismissed them as the ramblings of overactive imaginations, the kind of tales spun to give life a dash of excitement. But on one fateful night, his scepticism would be shattered into a thousand pieces, and he would become a firsthand witness to the inexplicable horrors that lurked in the shadows.

It was a moonless night, the very air thick with a palpable sense of dread. Barry found himself walking alone on the deserted streets, an ominous hush settling over the town. The distant hum of factories and the soft rustling of leaves in the wind created an eerie symphony that seemed to be the prelude to something dark and foreboding.

As he meandered through the labyrinthine alleys of Darlaston, an overwhelming feeling of unease gnawed at him. His footsteps echoed through the narrow streets, the sound serving as a constant reminder of his solitude. The town, usually bustling with life during daylight hours, had transformed into a desolate maze of shadows and silence.

Barry's senses were heightened, his every nerve on edge, as he navigated the dimly lit streets. The faint glow of the streetlights cast elongated shadows that danced menacingly along the pavement. He couldn't shake the feeling that he was being watched, that unseen eyes followed his every move.

As he passed a particularly narrow and sinister alleyway, he noticed a peculiar movement out of the corner of his eye. At first, he dismissed it as a trick of the shadows, a fleeting illusion created by his frazzled nerves. But the movement persisted, growing bolder with each passing moment.

Unable to ignore it any longer, Barry turned his gaze toward the source of the disturbance. What he beheld in that surreal moment defied all reason and logic. There, beneath the flickering streetlight, he saw them – shadowy figures that seemed to materialise out of the darkness itself.

The figures moved with an otherworldly grace, their forms twisting and contorting as if engaged in a ghostly waltz. Their movements were fluid and ethereal, as if they were part of some spectral ballet that transcended the boundaries of life and death.

Barry's heart pounded in his chest as he watched in terror. He wanted to run, to flee from this surreal nightmare, but his feet felt like lead, rooted to the spot as if by some malevolent force. Paralyzed by fear, he could only watch in horror as the enigmatic figures continued their haunting dance.

These entities had no discernible features, just shifting masses of darkness that swirled and cavorted in the eerie silence of the night. It was a macabre display, a sinister waltz that defied all rational explanation.

The wind whispered through the alleyway, carrying with it an otherworldly tune, a haunting melody that sent shivers down Barry's spine. It was as if the very air itself had been imbued with a mournful lament, a dirge for the living who dared to bear witness to the supernatural.

Minutes turned into hours as Barry remained entranced by the surreal spectacle. He couldn't tear his eyes away from the waltzing shadows, and the world around him seemed to fade into obscurity. It was as if he had crossed into a realm where the boundaries between the living and the dead blurred, where the very essence of reality was called into question.

The spectral dance continued, the figures twirling and weaving through the inky darkness. They seemed oblivious to Barry's presence, lost in their own ethereal world. The wind carried their haunting whispers, a symphony of the damned that echoed through the alleyways.

As the first faint rays of dawn began to break over the horizon, the shadowy figures gradually dissipated, their dance coming to an end. The street returned to its normal, mundane appearance, as if nothing out of the ordinary had occurred. The world had shifted back into its regular rhythm, but Barry knew that he could never truly return to the life he had known before.

Released from his trance, Barry stumbled back from the alleyway, his heart still racing, his mind in turmoil. He knew he could never truly explain what he had witnessed that night. It was a phenomenon beyond the realm of rationality, a glimpse into a world where the shadows themselves came to life, a world that lay hidden just beneath the surface of our own.

From that night forward, Barry was never the same. The dancing shadows of Darlaston haunted his every waking moment, a constant reminder of the eerie encounter that had shattered his scepticism and plunged him into a nightmarish reality. He had crossed a threshold into a realm of the unexplained, a world where the boundary between the living and the dead was no longer clear.

The townspeople of Darlaston continued to speak of the

spectral dance that graced their streets long after midnight. They knew that the shadows held secrets that could never be fully understood, and they walked the darkened streets with a mixture of trepidation and awe.

The legend of Darlaston's Dancing Shadows persisted, a chilling reminder that in the heart of the Black Country, the line between reality and the supernatural was as thin as a wisp of smoke, and the darkness held mysteries that defied explanation. The residents of Darlaston dared not wander the streets alone at night, for they knew that the spectral dance could claim anyone who strayed too close to the abyss of the unknown.

THE COSELEY CLOCK SPECTER

In the heart of Coseley, a quiet and historic town in the Black Country, an enigma had gripped the community for generations. It was an eerie mystery that seemed to belong to a world beyond our own, hiding in the shadows and defying explanation.

Danielle, a local resident with roots deeply entwined with Coseley's history, had always been fascinated by the town's timeless charm. Its cobblestone streets and centuries-old buildings were witnesses to the passage of countless years. Yet, amid this historical tapestry, one relic stood out—the ancient clock that adorned a small, unassuming structure.

This grand clock, a sentinel of time that had presided over the town for longer than memory could recount, was as much a source of comfort as it was an enigma. Its chimes, once a dependable marker of the hours, had become harbingers of the uncanny.

The mystery revolved around the inexplicable chimes. Instead of striking the hours as the hands of the clock dictated, it chimed at odd, irregular intervals, seeming to disregard the laws of time itself. In the deep stillness of night, when the world slumbered, the haunting notes of the clock would resonate through the town, stirring unease and restlessness.

The people of Coseley had grown accustomed to this spectral atmosphere that now enveloped their lives. Each eerie chime was accompanied by the appearance of a shadowy figure beneath the clock's towering presence—a figure that seemed to emerge from the very depths of the night.

This enigmatic figure, a shape obscured by darkness, held a silent vigil beneath the ancient timepiece. It was a presence shrouded in mystery, one that left the townsfolk in a perpetual state of unease.

Danielle, like many others, had been a witness to this apparition on numerous occasions. It was as though the figure was inexorably linked to the clock's haunting chimes, an eerie presence that had come to haunt the town's nights.

One moonless night, driven by a mixture of fear and curiosity that had gripped her for so long, Danielle ventured to the small structure that housed the clock. As the chimes reverberated through the air, she approached with trepidation, her heart pounding in her chest.

The shadowy figure, just as she remembered, stood beneath the ancient timepiece. It was a tall, spectral presence, its form ever-elusive, like an absence given shape—a void within the semblance of a man.

"Who are you?" Danielle called out, her voice wavering with a potent mixture of fear and fascination.

There was no response, just an oppressive silence that seemed to thicken the night air. The figure remained motionless, as though trapped in an eternal moment. Danielle's curiosity overcame her fear, compelling her to draw nearer, to seek the truth behind this enigma.

With each step, the figure seemed to waver, its form shifting like smoke in the wind. As Danielle's trembling hand reached out to touch it, she was met with a surreal sensation—her fingers passed through the figure as if it were an insubstantial mist, a phantom without substance.

Then, as abruptly as it had appeared, the figure dissipated

into the night, vanishing into the obscurity from which it had emerged. The clock's chimes ceased, and Danielle was left standing alone beneath the ancient timepiece, her heart racing, her mind brimming with both trepidation and wonder.

To this day, the clock in Coseley continues to chime at inexplicable hours, and the shadowy figure lingers nearby. It is a riddle that has haunted the town for generations, a spectral presence that remains beyond the grasp of human understanding.

Danielle and her fellow residents live with the knowledge that some mysteries are destined to remain unsolved, and that within the depths of the night, the boundary between the living and the supernatural grows tantalisingly thin.

But as the years passed, the haunting of Coseley took on an even more sinister aspect. Residents began to report disturbing dreams and nightmarish visions, each one more unsettling than the last. It was as though the town itself had become a portal to a realm of unfathomable darkness.

In these visions, they saw the shadowy figure, not as a distant spectre, but as a malevolent entity that sought to draw them into its grasp. They felt its icy fingers brush against their skin, sending shivers down their spines, and heard its chilling whispers, like the echoes of a thousand tormented souls.

The once-cosy streets of Coseley now felt oppressive, and the townsfolk became prisoners of their own homes, afraid to venture out after dark. Sleep became a torment, for in the realm of dreams, they were confronted by the relentless presence of the clock and the shadowy figure that lurked beneath it.

Desperation grew, and a deep-seated fear settled over Coseley like a suffocating fog. The townspeople searched for answers, turning to local legends and tales of the supernatural. Some believed that the clock was a cursed relic, a conduit to a realm of malevolence that defied human understanding.

As the torment continued, a collective sense of dread enveloped the town. It was as though Coseley itself had become a haunted place, its very soul tainted by the sinister presence that had taken root beneath the ancient clock.

And so, the enigma of Coseley endured, a chilling tale of a town plagued by an otherworldly malevolence that defied explanation. The clock continued to chime at odd hours, and the shadowy figure lingered in the nightmares of those who called Coseley home. In the depths of night, the boundary between the living and the supernatural remained tantalisingly thin, a dark mystery that refused to yield its secrets.

BROWNHILLS' BEWILDERING BOATMAN

Deep within the heart of Brownhills, a once-thriving mining community cradled amidst the sprawling industrial tapestry of the Black Country, an enduring and spine-tingling legend weaved its eerie thread through the annals of time. This tale was not merely a whisper in the wind; it was a spectral narrative that defied the boundaries of human comprehension and reason.

James and Rita, a couple in the twilight of middle age with a shared penchant for the enigmatic and the unexplained, had oft heard the hushed murmurs of this unsettling legend from their fellow townsfolk. This particular narrative spun the eerie yarn of a spectral figure, an otherworldly boatman who, under the concealing veil of the night, could be glimpsed plying his phantom craft upon a long-vanished lake, a body of water erased from the very fabric of existence.

In a bygone era, this lake had stood as the shimmering jewel of Brownhills—a tranquil oasis nestled amidst the bleak and formidable backdrop of the coal mines. Its placid waters had mirrored the stillness that lay far beneath the ground, offering solace and respite to those whose lives were a ceaseless dance in the subterranean labyrinth.

But, as the ceaseless wheels of industrialization forged their relentless path through the region, the lake's fate had been sealed. It was drained, filled, and consigned to oblivion, sacrificed upon the altar of ceaseless progress, a symbol of the voracious appetite of development.

Yet, the legend of the boatman refused to surrender to the

inexorable march of time. It endured, passed down through the generations as a shadow that clung tenaciously to the town's history. As the moon climbed high into the night sky, casting an eerie luminescence over the world, and the realm was draped in the inky shroud of darkness, the spectral boatman was rumoured to emerge once more, returning to ply his spectral trade.

On one fateful evening, curiosity lured James and Rita from the warmth and comfort of their home. The sun dipped below the horizon, casting long, gnarled shadows across the land. It was at that precise moment, when the remnants of daylight surrendered to the encroaching night, that the spectral boatman materialised before their very eyes.

He came into being as though born of the very substance of the night itself—a figure enshrouded in a ghostly mist, his features obscured by an ethereal veil that cloaked him from head to toe. The rowboat he commanded was every bit as spectral, its oars cutting through the air with a haunting resonance that sent shivers coursing down the spines of James and Rita.

The boatman's passage across the spectral waters was a macabre ballet of shadows and unearthly light, a performance that flouted the conventions of the natural world. With each measured stroke of his oars, the boat appeared to traverse an unseen dimension, conjuring ripples that reverberated in a realm beyond mortal perception.

James and Rita stood rooted to the spot, their hearts gripped by a potent sense of foreboding that refused to release its hold. The spectral lake, though banished from the realm of the living, sprang to ghostly life with each rhythmic pull of the oars, as if it harboured arcane secrets that transcended the boundaries of reality itself.

As the boatman continued his spectral odyssey, a profound melancholy descended upon the couple—a mournful lament that seemed to emanate from the very soul of Brownhills, a lamentation that encapsulated the town's history, its triumphs, and its tribulations.

When the boatman's spectral voyage at last drew to its enigmatic conclusion, he simply dissolved into the mists, his figure fading into the obsidian veil of the night. James and Rita were left standing in the profound silence of the darkness, haunted by the profound encounter they had been granted.

They knew, in the marrow of their bones, that the legend of the Brownhills boatman would endure, passed down through the ages as a testament to the enduring connection between the town's storied past and its enigmatic present. In the very heart of the Black Country, where history and the supernatural wove their eerie tapestry, the spectral boatman would forever ply his phantom trade upon the lake of memory, a vigilant guardian of the town's timeless legacy, a sentinel of the unexplainable and the otherworldly.

ECHOES OF CRADLEY HEATH

In the heart of Cradley Heath, a town nestled amidst the storied landscape of the Black Country, there existed a legend that transcended the bounds of ordinary tales. It was a spectral narrative, a chilling enigma that wove itself into the very fabric of the town's history—an enigmatic haunting that refused to be confined to the annals of time.

Amongst the townsfolk, stories of this legend had been whispered from one generation to the next, shared in hushed tones and with solemn reverence. The tale told of ancient battles, of spectral reenactments that unfolded on certain fateful nights beneath the silver glow of the moon. What set this legend apart from others was the eerie accompaniment of ghostly war cries that reverberated through the very marrow of those who bore witness.

These spectral skirmishes, it was said, transpired when the moon, luminous and full, hung high in the ink-dark canvas of the night sky. On such nights, when the very air seemed to thrum with an otherworldly energy, Kalvin, a resident of Cradley Heath with a fervent fascination for the mysterious and uncanny, found himself compelled to test the veracity of these chilling tales.

One moonlit evening, as the midnight hour approached, Kalvin ventured to the very heart of Cradley Heath—a place steeped in history and seeped in the echoes of its turbulent past. He stood atop a hill that had borne witness to fierce battles centuries ago, where the soil had absorbed the bloodshed and the air had carried the lamentations of warriors.

The night was awash in an eerie silence, the stillness broken only by the faint rustle of leaves in the nocturnal breeze. As the clock's hands inched towards midnight, Kalvin, his heart pounding with a mix of trepidation and anticipation, gazed out over the hallowed ground.

Suddenly, a spectral mist began to rise from the earth, enveloping the battlefield like a shroud of ethereal smoke. It was as though the very land retained the memory of its violent history—a history that was about to be replayed before Kalvin's disbelieving eyes.

From within the ghostly haze emerged the echoes of ancient battles. Shadowy warriors materialised on the field, their armour and weapons gleaming with an otherworldly lustre. With each step, they moved with a grace that defied mortal understanding, their spectral forms imbued with an unsettling, fluid quality.

The clash of ghostly weapons reverberated through the night, creating an eerie symphony of combat. The warriors' war cries, haunting and mournful, pierced the darkness, their voices carrying the weight of lives lived and lost in the turmoil of war.

Kalvin watched in awe and terror as the spectral reenactment played out before him. The warriors fought with a ferocity that bespoke of ancient grievances, their movements mirroring a dance of death that spanned the chasm of time.

The very air grew heavy with the acrid scent of battle—a stench that lingered as a testament to the violence that had once stained the ground. The combatants paid no heed to Kalvin; he was but an inconspicuous observer, an unseen guest to a gruesome performance scripted by history itself.

As the spectral battle reached its climactic crescendo, the war cries of the ghostly warriors reached a deafening, almost unbearable pitch. It was a crescendo of suffering, an eerie lamentation that resonated with the poignancy of lives cut short and destinies left unfulfilled.

Then, as abruptly as it had begun, the spectral reenactment dissolved into the misty ether. The battlefield returned to its tranquil, moonlit serenity, and Kalvin stood alone amid the aftermath of the spectral conflict. His heart still raced, his senses still heightened by the visceral intensity of the encounter.

He understood that the legend of Cradley Heath's spectral battles would persist, enduring through the generations as a reminder of the town's tumultuous past—a past fraught with strife and sacrifice. In the heart of the Black Country, where history and the supernatural converged, the echoes of ancient battles would continue to replay on certain nights, complete with ghostly war cries—a poignant and eerie testament to the enduring power of the past.

THE AMBLECOTE
APPARITION

In the quaint village of Amblecote, nestled within the historic heart of the Black Country, there was a spectral tale that had woven itself into the very fabric of the community—a story of an ethereal woman in white whose haunting presence was both a harbinger of hope and a harbinger of doom.

The villagers, generation after generation, had whispered the legend of Mary, the lady in white who walked by the river's edge. Her spectral figure, shrouded in a luminous gown, would often appear on moonlit nights, her presence casting an eerie, ethereal glow across the tranquil waters.

It was said that Mary was a guardian of hidden treasures, known only to those who followed her ethereal lead. But the path she guided them along was fraught with uncertainty, and the rewards she promised came with a price—an ominous price that sent shivers down the spines of those who dared to seek her out.

On one fateful night, John, a curious villager with a streak of adventure coursing through his veins, decided to test the veracity of the legend. Drawn by the allure of treasure and the mystique of the lady in white, he ventured to the riverbank as the moon ascended to its zenith.

The night was eerily silent, the air thick with an uncanny stillness that seemed to herald Mary's imminent appearance. As the first glimmers of her ghostly figure emerged, John's heart quickened, and his pulse raced in anticipation.

Mary, clad in her luminous white gown, moved with an

otherworldly grace as she glided along the riverbank. Her pale visage bore an ethereal beauty that both captivated and unnerved those who beheld her.

Without uttering a word, she beckoned to John with a graceful gesture, her spectral hand extended toward the darkness beyond. The moonlight caught the twinkle in her eyes, offering a glimpse of the secrets she held.

Unable to resist the siren's call, John followed Mary into the night, stepping into the shadows cast by her haunting presence. They ventured deeper into the woods, where moonbeams filtered through the leaves like a spectral canopy.

With each step, John felt a growing sense of unease, as though the very forest itself were closing in around them. The night sounds, once distant and benign, took on an eerie quality, filling the air with an unsettling chorus of whispers and murmurs.

As they journeyed further into the darkness, Mary led John to the entrance of an ancient, overgrown mine. The entrance, long abandoned and concealed by the passage of time, bore an air of foreboding that sent a shiver down John's spine.

Without hesitation, Mary descended into the depths of the mine, her luminous gown casting an eerie radiance that illuminated the subterranean passage. John, overcome by both fear and fascination, followed her into the abyss.

Inside the mine, the air grew colder, and the oppressive silence was broken only by the faint drip of water echoing through the tunnels. Mary moved with purpose, her ethereal glow guiding John deeper into the subterranean labyrinth.

Finally, they reached a chamber bathed in an otherworldly light. In the centre of the chamber lay a trove of gleaming riches— gold, jewels, and precious artefacts that sparkled like stars in the spectral glow.

The sight was mesmerising, and John's greed overcame his sense of caution. He reached out to claim the treasure, but before his fingers could make contact, Mary's spectral form shifted and contorted, revealing a nightmarish countenance.

Her once-beautiful face twisted into a grotesque mask, her eyes now hollow and soulless. Her ethereal gown transformed into a suffocating shroud, ensnaring John with spectral tendrils that coiled around him like serpents.

In a haunting chorus, the tormented voices of those who had been ensnared before him echoed through the chamber. Their wails of despair and suffering filled John's ears, drowning out his own terrified cries.

With a sudden, violent jerk, Mary pulled John into her ghostly embrace, and he felt himself being drawn into the darkness. The chamber's spectral light faded, and the treasures vanished into nothingness.

The legend of Mary, the lady in white by the river, endured in the village of Amblecote, but now it carried a chilling warning. Those who dared to seek her out were met with a fate worse than any imagined wealth could provide—a fate entwined with the anguish of the countless souls who had been lured by her spectral allure.

In the heart of the Black Country, where legends and the supernatural converged, the Amblecote Apparition continued to walk the river's edge, both a beacon of spectral beauty and a harbinger of eternal darkness.

NETHERTON'S NIGHTLY KNOCK

In the heart of Netherton, a quiet suburb nestled amidst the labyrinthine streets of the Black Country, there existed a spectral enigma that had baffled residents for generations—an eerie phenomenon known as "Netherton's Nightly Knock." This haunting tale whispered of a mysterious, repetitive knock that would manifest on the doors of homes under the cover of night, leaving those who experienced it in a state of dread and bewilderment.

Harold, a middle-aged man known for his scepticism and rationality, had always dismissed the stories of the Nightly Knock as mere superstition. He believed that there must be a logical explanation for the eerie occurrences that occasionally befell the residents of Netherton. After all, he reasoned, modern life had little room for the inexplicable.

One evening, however, as Harold reclined in his cosy living room, a sense of unease began to gnaw at him. The night outside was unusually still, the air heavy with an eerie calm. It was during this uncanny stillness that Harold heard it—a sharp, deliberate knock emanating from his front door.

Startled, he sat upright, his heart quickening its pace. The knock came again, three slow and deliberate raps that reverberated through the silent house. There was an unsettling rhythm to it, like a macabre dance of some unseen presence in the dark.

Harold, filled with a mixture of curiosity and trepidation, cautiously approached the door. He peered through the peephole, expecting to find a neighbour or perhaps a lost traveller seeking directions. To his astonishment, there was no one there—only the empty, dimly lit street shrouded in an unnatural fog.

The unsettling knock continued, each rap echoing through the house as though it originated from the very walls themselves. It persisted for hours, a relentless, maddening drumbeat that seemed to mock Harold's attempts to locate its source.

Desperate for answers, he flung open the door, expecting to confront a prankster or a wandering soul in need of assistance. To his dismay, the empty street greeted him, devoid of any living presence. The knock, however, continued, now echoing through the darkness beyond.

Harold's rationality crumbled in the face of this inexplicable phenomenon. He retreated inside, determined to find the source of the spectral disturbance that had invaded his home. But no matter where he searched, he found no origin for the relentless knocking, no rational explanation to soothe his racing mind.

As the hours stretched into the early morning, the spectral knock persisted, each rap growing louder and more insistent. The once-familiar comfort of Harold's home had transformed into a labyrinth of dread, where the walls themselves seemed to pulse with a malevolent energy.

With the first light of dawn, the haunting knock finally ceased. Harold, his nerves frayed and his mind in disarray, could scarcely believe the ordeal he had endured. He knew that he could no longer dismiss the tales of Netherton's Nightly Knock as mere superstition; he had become a witness to its chilling reality.

Over time, the legend of Netherton's Nightly Knock endured in the suburb, passed down through the generations as a testament to the enigmatic and inexplicable. Each resident who experienced the spectral phenomenon did so with a mixture of dread and fascination, their rationality forever shaken by the relentless, ghostly raps on their doors.

In Netherton, where the boundary between the natural and the supernatural was blurred, the Nightly Knock continued to haunt the night, a mysterious enigma that eluded all attempts at explanation.

As the years passed, Harold became something of a local legend himself, known as the man who had confronted the spectral knock and lived to tell the tale. He found himself drawn to the inexplicable, dedicating his nights to investigating the eerie happenings that plagued Netherton.

In his quest for answers, Harold discovered that the Nightly Knock was no isolated incident. Many residents had experienced the spectral phenomenon, and their accounts revealed a pattern. It appeared that the knock occurred most frequently on moonless nights, during the stillness of the small hours when the world slumbered.

Harold delved deeper into the history of Netherton, unearthing tales of the suburb's distant past. He discovered that the area had once been the site of ancient battles, where rival factions clashed in fierce combat. It was said that the ghostly knocks were echoes of those long-forgotten conflicts, as if the tumultuous events of the past had imprinted themselves on the very fabric of the suburb.

Undeterred by the eerie revelations, Harold sought to communicate with the restless spirits that seemed to be trapped in a perpetual cycle of conflict. Armed with recording equipment and a determination to uncover the truth, he embarked on a series of nocturnal vigils.

On one particularly dark night, Harold's efforts bore fruit. As he sat in the dim glow of candlelight, his recording devices captured a chorus of spectral whispers—an ethereal symphony of voices recounting tales of battle and anguish. It was as though the long-lost warriors had found a voice through Harold's endeavours.

The whispers spoke of ancient grievances, of battles fought over territory and honour, of lives cut short in the brutal chaos of war. They yearned for resolution, for acknowledgment of the past that bound them to Netherton's streets. In their ghostly voices, Harold sensed a profound sadness, a desire for closure that transcended the boundaries of life and death.

Determined to bring peace to the restless spirits, Harold embarked on a mission to commemorate the long-forgotten battles that had scarred Netherton's history. With the support of the community, he organised a memorial event, inviting residents to pay their respects to the fallen warriors of centuries past.

As the solemn ceremony unfolded beneath the moonless sky, a palpable sense of reverence filled the air. It was as though the spirits of the ancient warriors had gathered to bear witness to the acknowledgment of their sacrifice.

In the days that followed, the spectral knocks on Netherton's doors grew fainter and less frequent. It was as though the restless spirits, their stories finally heard and their battles acknowledged, had found a measure of peace. The legend of Netherton's Nightly Knock gradually faded into memory, a testament to the power of understanding and remembrance.

Harold, having played a pivotal role in uncovering the truth behind the enigmatic phenomenon, continued his work as a guardian of Netherton's history. He knew that beneath the quiet streets and modern façade of the suburb, echoes of the past still lingered, waiting to be heard by those who dared to listen.

WORDSLEY'S WINDOW WATCHER

In the quiet, forgotten corners of Wordsley, a small town nestled within the heart of the Black Country, there existed a spectral enigma that had long whispered through the annals of local lore. The eerie tale spoke of the "Wordsley Window Watcher," a phantom presence that frequently manifested in the window of an abandoned building, its eerie visage both haunting and enigmatic.

Terry and Mick, two friends who shared an insatiable curiosity for the unexplained, had often heard the unsettling stories that swirled around this spectral mystery. Wordsley had always been a town steeped in history, with abandoned buildings that bore witness to the passage of time. Among them, one structure stood out—an old, dilapidated house that had remained empty and desolate for as long as anyone could remember.

It was this forsaken building that held the secret of the Window Watcher. Locals claimed that, on certain moonless nights, a face would materialise in one of the tattered windows—a pale, ethereal countenance with hollow eyes that seemed to pierce through the veil between the living and the dead.

Terry and Mick, fueled by equal parts curiosity and trepidation, decided to venture to the abandoned house one fateful evening. The air was heavy with the weight of history as they approached the decaying structure. The building stood as a sentinel of a forgotten era, its windows long bereft of glass, its walls bearing the scars of time.

As the moon hid behind a shroud of thick clouds, casting

the night into an abyssal darkness, the friends reached the building's entrance. The doorway beckoned them with an eerie stillness that seemed to defy the world outside. With cautious steps, they entered the forsaken house, their flashlights casting feeble beams that revealed a place frozen in time.

The interior was as they had expected—an eerie tableau of decay and abandonment. Dust-covered furniture stood frozen in place, as if waiting for the return of occupants who had long since departed. Cobwebs hung like spectral veils, obscuring the passage of years.

Terry and Mick ascended the creaking staircase, their footsteps echoing through the empty halls. They reached the room where the spectral apparition was said to appear—a room with a single window overlooking the desolate street below.

As they stood in the dimly lit room, the atmosphere seemed to thicken with anticipation. The air grew colder, and the sound of their breathing was a ghostly echo in the stillness. It was then that, from the corner of their eyes, they glimpsed it—the pale face of the Wordsley Window Watcher.

The apparition was as described in the tales—a visage ethereal and unnerving, with hollow eyes that bore into the souls of those who dared to witness it. It remained motionless, framed in the decaying window, a silent sentinel of an enigmatic past.

Terry and Mick watched in awe and fear as the spectral face lingered, its presence casting a chilling pall over the room. It seemed to beckon them, to draw them into its haunting gaze, compelling them to question the boundaries of reality.

Time seemed to blur as the friends stood entranced, locked in a spectral communion with the enigmatic entity. They felt as though they had glimpsed a world beyond, a realm where the past and present converged in a haunting dance.

Then, as abruptly as it had appeared, the Wordsley Window

Watcher dissolved into the darkness. The room returned to its eerie stillness, leaving Terry and Mick in a state of bewildered wonder.

They descended the staircase, their minds reeling from the inexplicable encounter. The abandoned house, with its hidden mysteries and spectral secrets, had left an indelible mark on their souls. They knew that the legend of the Window Watcher would continue to haunt their thoughts, a testament to the enigma of Wordsley's forgotten past.

As they stepped out into the moonlit night, the abandoned building seemed to watch over them, its windows like dark eyes that concealed untold secrets. Terry and Mick had ventured into the realm of the unexplained, and in the heart of Wordsley, where history and the supernatural converged, the Window Watcher would forever remain an enigmatic guardian of the town's timeless mysteries.

Weeks passed since Terry and Mick's unsettling encounter with the Wordsley Window Watcher. The memory of that eerie night haunted their thoughts, leading them to seek answers where others might have chosen to forget. As the days grew shorter and the nights darker, the two friends embarked on a quest to unravel the enigma that had captivated their imaginations.

Their investigation began in the quiet corners of Wordsley's local library, where dusty volumes held records of the town's history. Terry and Mick were determined to discover any trace of the forsaken house and its mysterious inhabitant. Hours turned into days as they meticulously pored over old maps, land deeds, and faded photographs.

Their efforts bore fruit when they stumbled upon an old photograph—a sepia-toned image that depicted the very building they had explored. The photograph was dated, harkening back to the late 19th century when the house was a proud residence, inhabited by a family whose name had long been forgotten.

Further research revealed that the house had fallen into disrepair in the early 20th century, after the last living occupants had departed. Local rumours hinted at tragedies within its walls, though details were scarce.

The two friends also uncovered references to the spectral figure that had come to be known as the Wordsley Window Watcher. Tales of the ghostly presence dated back decades, with various witnesses recounting their eerie encounters. Some spoke of a mournful, whispering voice that accompanied the apparition, though others could offer no explanation for its presence.

Armed with historical insights, Terry and Mick continued their investigation into the paranormal occurrences surrounding the house. They reached out to local historians and residents who might have stories to share. Slowly, a tapestry of tales emerged— a patchwork of unexplained phenomena, from chilling whispers in the night to glimpses of shadowy figures within the abandoned house.

One particularly unsettling account came from an elderly resident who had grown up in the vicinity of the forsaken building. She recounted her childhood terror as she watched the spectral figure, the very same Wordsley Window Watcher, from her bedroom window. The apparition had not been limited to a single witness; it had been a recurring presence, casting a pall over the neighbourhood for generations.

Terry and Mick's quest for answers led them back to the abandoned house. Armed with an array of investigative tools, including cameras, audio recording devices, and electromagnetic field metres, they embarked on a series of nocturnal vigils.

Their first vigil was met with eerie silence. The old house stood as it had on previous visits, a brooding sentinel of the past. The spectral face did not materialise in the window, leaving Terry and Mick in a state of uncertainty.

Undeterred, they returned to the house night after night, their determination unshaken. It was during their third vigil that something inexplicable occurred. As the moon hung low in the night sky, casting an ethereal glow upon the abandoned building, the room containing the spectral window revealed its secret.

A faint, whispering voice filled the room—a voice that seemed to emanate from the very walls themselves. Terry and Mick recorded the eerie sounds, capturing disembodied whispers and murmurs that defied explanation. It was as if the house itself held the memories of its past, memories that whispered through the corridors of time.

The friends also captured anomalous readings on their electromagnetic field metres, registering fluctuations that seemed to defy the laws of nature. Unexplained cold spots manifested in the room, casting shadows that danced like spectres.

During one vigil, as Terry and Mick focused their attention on the window, a series of knocks echoed through the room, each knock growing louder and more insistent. They quickly ruled out any rational explanation—no drafts, no external sources of sound. The knocks were otherworldly, an enigmatic message from a presence beyond.

As the months passed, Terry and Mick's findings deepened the enigma of the Wordsley Window Watcher. Their investigations led them to believe that the apparition was more than a mere ghostly figure—it was a manifestation of a past steeped in mysteries, a past that refused to fade into obscurity.

The spectral face that had haunted their initial encounter remained elusive, appearing only sporadically. Yet, the friends could sense a growing connection, a bridge between the living and the spectral. They believed that the entity sought to communicate, to share its untold stories with those who dared to listen.

Terry and Mick's journey into the heart of the unexplained had only just begun. The Wordsley Window Watcher, with its secrets and whispers, remained an enduring enigma—an ethereal guardian of the town's mysteries, a timeless presence that linked the past to the present, and a testament to the enduring allure of the unknown in the quiet corners of the Black Country.

THE PELSALL POLTERGEIST

In the tranquil village of Pelsall, nestled amidst the serene landscapes of the Black Country, an enigmatic legend lay shrouded in the mists of time—a legend that defied explanation and sent shivers down the spines of those who dared to ponder its mysteries. It was a tale of a spectral presence known as the Pelsall Poltergeist, an entity that walked the fine line between the realms of the living and the dead.

Craig, a man with an insatiable curiosity and a deep reverence for the past, had heard the whispers of this unsettling legend during his many visits to the village's historic haunts. Pelsall was a place where the echoes of history reverberated through its timeworn buildings, a town where the past and present existed in a delicate dance.

The house in question, nestled at the heart of the village, was a testament to a bygone era. Generations of a single family had called it home, and as the years had passed, so too had the unsettling presence within its walls grown in prominence. It was as if the house itself held secrets that had transcended time.

Craig had often heard tales of strange occurrences within the house—a whispering wind that carried a name on its breath, the inexplicable movement of objects as if guided by unseen hands, and an air of melancholy that hung like a shroud. But it was the chair that slid of its own volition that had piqued his curiosity.

One evening, as twilight cast long shadows over Pelsall, Craig found himself drawn to the historic house like a moth to a flame. The air grew chill as he approached, and a sense of unease settled upon him. He pushed open the creaking door, its timeworn wood offering little resistance.

The room was cloaked in an eerie silence, broken only by the faint ticking of an antique clock. Craig's breath hung in the air like a mist as he ventured further into the dimly lit space. The chair, unoccupied and yet seemingly alive, stood as a testament to the uncanny.

With bated breath, Craig watched as the chair began its otherworldly dance. It slid across the wooden floor, its legs scraping softly, guided by an unseen force. The room seemed to hum with a spectral energy, and Craig felt as though he had stepped into a realm where the boundaries of reality blurred.

As the chair moved, Craig's eyes were drawn to the adjacent mirror—an ancient looking glass that seemed to hold its own secrets. As he approached, a sudden gust of cold air enveloped him, its touch unnatural and unsettling.

In the mirror's reflection, Craig saw himself, but there was something more—a presence lurking in the shadows behind him. A figure, ethereal and haunting, materialised before his eyes. Hollow eyes, filled with an otherworldly sadness, bore into Craig's soul.

The room seemed to tremble with a spectral presence as the figure reached out from the mirror, its translucent hand passing through the glass as if to bridge the gap between the living and the dead. A profound sense of foreboding washed over Craig as he met the spectral gaze of the Pelsall Poltergeist.

In that moment, he realised that this was not a malevolent entity but a presence that sought to communicate, to convey a message from beyond the veil. The room reverberated with an otherworldly energy, and Craig's heart raced as he stood on the precipice of the unexplained.

With a final, mournful whisper, the spirit faded into the shadows, leaving Craig standing alone in the attic, haunted by the encounter he had borne witness to. The house in Pelsall, with its timeworn walls and enigmatic past, had become a place where history and the supernatural converged in a dance of the unexplained.

As he stepped out into the moonlit night, the old house watched over him, its windows like dark eyes that concealed untold secrets. Craig knew that the legend of the Pelsall Poltergeist would endure, passed down through generations as a testament to the enduring connection between the living and the spectral. In the heart of Pelsall, where history and the supernatural converged, the Pelsall Poltergeist would forever remain an enigmatic guardian of the village's timeless mysteries, a link between the past and the present, bridging the realms of the known and the unknowable.

THE BARSTON LAKE LADY

In the heart of the Black Country, where time seemed to stand still amidst the remnants of a bygone era, there existed a place known as Barston Lake. Its tranquil waters, framed by ancient willows and overgrown reeds, held a tale as old as the land itself —a tale of love and loss, of a ghostly presence that had lingered through the ages.

Rachel, a young woman with a penchant for history and an affinity for the supernatural, had often heard hushed whispers of the spectral lady of Barston Lake. It was a story that captured her imagination, a story of love unfulfilled and a spirit forever bound by the chains of longing.

The legend spoke of a lady from a time long past, a time when Barston Lake had been a place of beauty and serenity, untouched by the relentless march of industry. In those days, the lady had been the belle of the village, her beauty and grace the talk of the town.

Her heart, however, had belonged to a dashing young man named Samuel, a millworker whose rugged charm had stolen her affections. Their love had blossomed amidst the idyllic backdrop of the lake, their stolen moments of togetherness by the water's edge etching memories of a love that defied the constraints of their social station.

But fate had a cruel twist in store for the young lovers. Samuel was called away to fight in a distant war, leaving behind a tearful promise to return to his beloved. The lady, heartbroken but resolute, had vowed to wait for him by the lake's shore, counting the days until their reunion.

The seasons turned, and the years passed, yet Samuel did not return. The lady, her raven hair now streaked with silver, continued her vigil by the lake, her eyes searching the horizon for a sight of her lost love. Villagers spoke of her unwavering devotion, of her hauntingly beautiful visage, and of the whispered conversations they heard her engaged in during the lonely nights.

Rachel, driven by an insatiable curiosity, ventured to the shores of Barston Lake one moonlit evening. The air grew heavy with a sense of melancholy as she approached the water's edge. The lake, once a haven of serenity, now seemed to hold the weight of a love story left unfinished.

As Rachel gazed upon the still waters, a shimmering figure materialised before her—a lady in a gown as white as the moonlight itself. Her long, ebony hair cascaded over her shoulders, and her eyes, filled with an eternal longing, met Rachel's with a mournful gaze.

The lady's ethereal form seemed to flicker in the moon's glow, her presence both haunting and mesmerising. Rachel, overcome by a profound sense of empathy, could feel the depths of the lady's sorrow, the unfulfilled promise of a love lost to the sands of time.

In that fleeting moment, the lady's spectral lips parted, and a soft, melodic voice escaped—a voice that sang of love, of longing, and of an eternity spent waiting for a lover who would never return. The mournful melody seemed to hang in the air, carrying with it the weight of a love story left unfinished.

With a final, ethereal sigh, the lady of Barston Lake faded back into the moonlight, leaving Rachel standing alone by the water's edge, haunted by the encounter she had just witnessed. She knew then that the legend of the Barston Lake lady would continue to endure, passed down through generations as a testament to the enduring power of love and the profound depths of sorrow. In the heart of the Black Country, where history and the supernatural converged, the lady would forever wait by the lake's shore, a spectral guardian of a love story that transcended the boundaries of time and mortality.

Rachel became obsessed with the tale of the Barston Lake lady. She spent countless hours researching the history of the village, scouring dusty archives and speaking to the eldest residents who held the memories of generations past. As she delved deeper into the story, she uncovered a wealth of details that added layers of complexity to the haunting legend.

It was said that the lady and Samuel had been childhood sweethearts, their love blossoming amidst the quaint charm of the village. They had shared stolen kisses beneath the willow trees that lined the lake's edge, their laughter echoing through the tranquil surroundings.

When Samuel received his call to serve in the war, the lady had gifted him a locket—a delicate piece of jewellery that held a miniature portrait of her. It was a token of her love and a promise that she would be with him in spirit, no matter the distance that separated them.

Samuel had treasured the locket throughout his time on the battlefield, finding solace in the image of his beloved whenever the horrors of war threatened to overwhelm him. He had shared stories of her beauty and grace with his fellow soldiers, painting a vivid picture of the lady who held his heart.

In the midst of a fierce battle, as the world exploded into chaos and violence, Samuel's life was tragically cut short. His comrades, bearing witness to his final moments, later recounted his dying words—a whispered declaration of love for the lady of Barston Lake.

Back in the village, the lady had felt a sudden, overwhelming grief wash over her. She had known, in the depths of her heart, that her beloved Samuel was no more. As if bound by an otherworldly connection, she had wept for him, her tears mingling with the waters of the lake that had been witness to their love.

With each passing day, the lady's grief had intensified, and her yearning for Samuel had grown stronger. She had ventured to the lake each night, hoping against hope that he would return to her as he had promised. Her whispers, carried by the wind, had become an eternal lament for a love that could never be rekindled.

Rachel's research led her to a collection of letters exchanged between Samuel and the lady during his time at war. The heartfelt words penned on yellowed pages spoke of a love that transcended time and distance, a love that had endured even in the face of death.

One particular letter, penned by Samuel on the eve of a fateful battle, had struck a chord in Rachel's heart. In it, he had expressed his undying love for the lady and his fervent hope that they would one day be reunited in the afterlife. The letter had never reached its intended recipient, but its discovery had added a poignant layer to the tale.

Determined to honour the memory of the lovers, Rachel organised a community event by Barston Lake, inviting villagers to gather and pay tribute to the lady and Samuel. Lanterns were lit along the water's edge, their warm glow reflecting in the still waters of the lake. The village choir sang hauntingly beautiful songs, and Rachel read aloud the letters exchanged by the lovers, their words carrying across the lake like a gentle breeze.

As the night wore on, something remarkable happened. A soft, ethereal glow appeared on the surface of the lake, a shimmering light that seemed to dance in time with the music. Gasps of astonishment rippled through the crowd as the spectral figure of the lady materialised on the water, her gown as white as the moonlight.

With a voice that carried a lifetime of longing, the lady sang a mournful melody, her words echoing the sentiments of the letters that had been read. It was a song of love, of loss, and of an unbreakable bond that even death could not sever.

Tears streamed down Rachel's cheeks as she watched the spectral performance, the beauty of the moment almost too much to bear. The villagers stood in reverent silence, their hearts heavy with the weight of the love story that had unfolded before them.

As the final notes of the song faded into the night, the lady of Barston Lake bowed her head in a gesture of farewell. With a soft, wistful sigh, she dissolved back into the moonlight, leaving behind a profound sense of peace and closure.

The villagers returned to their homes, their hearts touched by the beauty of the evening's tribute. Rachel knew that the legend of the lady of Barston Lake would continue to be passed down through generations, not as a tale of sorrow, but as a testament to the enduring power of love.

In the heart of the Black Country, where history and the supernatural converged, the lady would forever wait by the lake's shore, her love story a beacon of hope and remembrance for all who heard its haunting melody.

RUSHALL'S RESTLESS RIDER

In the quiet village of Rushall, nestled amidst the rolling hills of the Black Country, a tale of the supernatural had long lingered in the shadows—a legend that whispered of eerie apparitions and spectral guardians. It was a chilling story that transcended time and reason, and it began not with fear, but with the mysterious allure of a treasure hidden in the heart of the village.

Rushall, once a thriving mining community, had a history steeped in the riches of the earth. Its coal mines had been the lifeblood of the village, fueling its prosperity and shaping the destinies of its residents. But alongside the promise of wealth, the mines had also given rise to a tragic tale of betrayal, vengeance, and a curse that would bind the village to the supernatural for generations.

Among the newcomers to Rushall were Darren and Stephanie, a young couple seeking a fresh start in the tranquil embrace of the countryside. Blissfully unaware of the village's sinister past, they had been drawn to the picturesque landscape and the promise of a quaint, idyllic life.

Their new cottage, nestled amid the lush greenery of the hills, provided the perfect retreat from the bustling city life they had left behind. As they settled into their new surroundings, they discovered that Rushall was a place where time seemed to move at a different pace—a place where the past whispered in the rustling leaves of ancient trees and the babbling brooks that wound through the village.

Among their new neighbours was an elderly woman named Eliza, who, with her weathered face and eyes that held the weight of the years, had a tale to tell—one that would change

Darren and Stephanie's lives forever. She invited the young couple to her cosy cottage one evening, the warm glow of her hearth casting dancing shadows on the walls.

Over cups of steaming tea, Eliza spoke of the legend that had haunted Rushall for centuries. It was a tale of a treasure hidden deep within the village, a treasure that had been the source of both envy and treachery among the miners who had toiled beneath the earth's surface.

Eliza's voice trembled as she recounted the events of a fateful night—a night when greed had driven a group of miners to betray their comrades and seize the treasure for themselves. The ensuing violence had stained the earth with blood, and the curse that had descended upon Rushall had bound their restless spirits to the village for all eternity.

But it was not the tale of violence and betrayal that had piqued Darren and Stephanie's interest—it was the promise of a hidden treasure, one that had eluded the grasp of countless treasure hunters who had ventured into the depths of Rushall in search of fortune.

The couple, their curiosity piqued, listened intently as Eliza revealed the legend of the guardian of the treasure—a spectral figure, a headless horseman, who had been cursed to protect the riches from those who sought to claim them.

As the night grew darker and the flames in the hearth flickered, Eliza cautioned Darren and Stephanie against seeking the treasure, warning them of the malevolent spirit that guarded it. But the lure of untold wealth proved irresistible, and the couple's imaginations were ignited by the promise of adventure.

Under the cloak of night, with the moon casting an eerie pallor over the village, Darren and Stephanie set out on their quest. Armed with lanterns and shovels, they descended into the ancient mines that riddled Rushall's underground labyrinth.

The air grew cold and damp as they ventured deeper into the subterranean darkness, the walls of the mine bearing witness to the toil and sacrifice of generations past. It was a treacherous journey, filled with ominous echoes and the sense that they were not alone.

As they delved deeper into the bowels of the earth, they began to hear the faint sound of hoofbeats echoing through the tunnels —a rhythmic, haunting sound that seemed to draw closer with each step they took. The oppressive darkness was broken only by the dim light of their lanterns, casting long, wavering shadows on the walls.

Stephanie clung to Darren's arm, her heart pounding with a mixture of fear and excitement. It was then that they saw it —the spectral figure of the headless horseman, mounted on a ghostly steed, bearing down upon them with a malevolent determination.

The lanterns flickered and sputtered as the phantom rider drew near, his eyes, or the spaces where eyes should have been, glowing with an unholy light. His spectral form seemed to waver in and out of existence, as if he straddled the line between the living and the dead.

The headless horseman's presence was suffused with an aura of vengeance, his very essence a manifestation of the violence and betrayal that had cursed Rushall. As he drew closer, his unearthly wail echoed through the tunnels, a haunting lament that reverberated in the souls of Darren and Stephanie.

In a panic, the couple turned and fled, their footsteps pounding on the uneven ground. The headless horseman pursued them relentlessly, his unearthly steed keeping pace with their every stride. It was a race against the spectral rider, a battle of wills between the living and the dead.

Just as they reached the safety of Rushall's boundaries, the headless horseman reared up, his ghostly form dissipating into the night like smoke on the wind. Darren and Stephanie, gasping for breath and hearts pounding, collapsed onto the ground, their encounter with the supernatural seared into their memories.

From that night on, they knew that the legend of Rushall's restless rider was no mere superstition—it was a chilling reality that lurked in the shadows of the Black Country. The headless horseman, cursed to guard his cursed treasure for all eternity, would forever haunt the outskirts of Rushall, a spectre of vengeance and terror.

In the heart of the Black Country, where history and the supernatural converged, the restless rider would continue his eternal patrol, a sentinel of the cursed riches that lay hidden beneath the earth, waiting for the next unwitting souls who dared to challenge his spectral vigil.

THE SPECTER OF HIMLEY

In the heart of the enchanting Himley village, nestled amidst the verdant landscapes of the Black Country, an imposing structure known as Himley Hall stood as a silent witness to centuries of history. Its stately architecture and sprawling parklands made it a jewel of the region, attracting both locals and tourists alike.

Sophie, an intrepid soul with an insatiable curiosity for the macabre, had long heard whispers of Himley Hall's haunted reputation. The locals, too superstitious to venture near, dared not approach its grand facade. But Sophie was different; she sought the truth, no matter how unsettling it may be.

One storm-laden evening, as the heavens unleashed torrents of rain upon the Himley countryside, Sophie's fascination with the hall reached its zenith. The thunderclaps resonated like cannon fire, and the lightning illuminated the majestic mansion in stark, eerie flashes. It was then that she made her decision to explore the legendary Himley Hall.

With a lantern in hand and trepidation in her heart, Sophie stepped across the threshold of the grand house. The air within was heavy, laden with the weight of centuries of secrets. The floorboards creaked beneath her feet, as if the very house protested her presence.

As Sophie ventured deeper into Himley Hall, the chilling drafts seemed to speak to her, whispering of long-forgotten tragedies and unspoken horrors. She could hear faint voices, spectral echoes of a past that refused to fade.

Then, in the dim light of her lantern, Sophie saw her—a ghostly figure, clad in tattered rags, standing at the foot of a grand staircase. The apparition's eyes, cold and empty, bore into Sophie's soul, and her mouth opened soundlessly as if attempting to speak.

Before Sophie could react, the ghostly figure raised a translucent hand, pointing a spectral finger towards the window. The wind howled outside, rattling the glass panes, and rain battered against the fragile barrier between the living and the dead.

Intrigued and terrified in equal measure, Sophie approached the window. It was then that she realised the ghostly figure's message. As the lightning flashed, Sophie saw a terrifying vision —a tempestuous storm of unimaginable fury, with dark clouds swirling ominously overhead.

The ghostly spectre seemed to convey a warning, not just of the impending tempest that threatened to engulf Himley Hall but also of the tempest that raged within. Sophie's heart raced as she comprehended the dual nature of the message—an omen of both meteorological and emotional turmoil.

With a final, mournful glance, the ghostly figure slowly dissipated into the very air, leaving Sophie alone with her ominous premonition. Her pulse quickened, and a sense of impending doom hung heavily in the air.

As Sophie fled from Himley Hall, the storm outside reached its zenith. Lightning fractured the sky, and thunderclaps seemed to shake the earth itself. The ghostly apparition's warning echoed in her mind, a haunting reminder that some truths, whether about the weather or the human heart, were best left undisturbed.

Back in the safety of her home, Sophie couldn't shake the encounter with the ghostly harbinger of storms. She couldn't ignore the creeping sense of dread that clawed at her. As the tempest outside raged on, she began to understand that the spectral messenger had revealed not only the turmoil in the heavens but also the turmoil within herself.

Days turned into weeks, and Sophie became obsessed with uncovering the history of Himley Hall and the stories of those who had inhabited it. She learned of a tragic love story that had unfolded within its walls, a love torn asunder by societal conventions and familial obligations.

As Sophie delved deeper into her research, she uncovered old letters and diaries that told of forbidden romances and broken hearts. She realised that the ghostly figure she had encountered was that of a young woman, a tragic lover who had died pining for the one she could never have.

With each revelation, the connection between Sophie and the spectral apparition deepened. She felt the woman's sorrow as her own, and her heart ached for the love that had been lost to time.

One fateful evening, as Sophie sat by the window of her cottage, the skies darkened once more, and the wind howled like a mournful dirge. She knew that the ghostly woman would appear again, her ethereal form haunting the grounds of Himley Hall.

As the first raindrops splattered against the glass, Sophie saw her—a spectral vision, the lady in white, standing by the same window where they had first met. Her mournful eyes met Sophie's, and her outstretched hand beckoned.

Tears welled in Sophie's eyes as she realised the truth—the ghostly woman wasn't warning her of impending storms; she was seeking solace and companionship. She longed for someone to hear her story, to understand the depth of her despair.

With trembling hands, Sophie opened the window, inviting the ghostly lady inside. As she did, a sense of peace washed over her, and she knew that by sharing her love and her pain, she could help the tormented spirit find release.

From that day forward, Sophie and the spectral lady became kindred spirits, sharing their stories in the quiet hours of the night. The storms that once filled Sophie with dread now served as a backdrop to their bittersweet conversations.

As time passed, the hauntings at Himley Hall ceased, and the village of Himley embraced the legend of the lady in white, forever immortalised as the ghost who found solace in the company of a compassionate soul.

In the heart of Himley, where history and the supernatural converged, Himley Hall continued to stand as a testament to love and loss, and Sophie remained its guardian, a bridge between the living and the dead, offering solace to a restless spirit who had found a friend in the stormy nights of the Black Country.

SHORT HEATH'S
SHIMMERING SPIRIT

In the quiet neighbourhood of Short Heath, nestled amidst the rich history of the Black Country, a chilling legend unfolded—a story that would remain hidden from the watchful eyes of the world.

Jane, a discreet and observant woman with a passion for photography, had always been drawn to Short Heath's unique charm. Its streets were lined with charming houses that held centuries of secrets, and each one seemed to harbour an untold story, waiting to be uncovered through her camera's lens.

One crisp autumn afternoon, Jane ventured out with her camera, the golden rays of the setting sun casting long shadows across the streets. The neighbourhood was tranquil, as if the buildings themselves held their breath, and the atmosphere buzzed with a sense of expectation.

As Jane wandered along the picturesque lanes, her camera intermittently clicked, capturing the timeless beauty that surrounded her. The ageing facades of the houses, the rustling leaves of ancient trees, and the play of sunlight through wrought-iron gates—each frame was a homage to the neighbourhood's rich history.

But then, something extraordinary began to transpire. As Jane reviewed the photos she had taken, she noticed a peculiar occurrence. In each image, amongst the familiar surroundings, a subtle, otherworldly shimmer emerged—a translucent figure that appeared out of thin air.

Initially, Jane dismissed it as an optical illusion or perhaps a camera malfunction. However, as she continued to take pictures, the ethereal presence became increasingly distinct, its form acquiring a ghostly shape, as if it were trying to convey a message from the hidden realms.

With every click, Jane's unease grew, and the figure, a shimmering spectre of indistinct gender, seemed to manifest in various poses within her photos, as though it sought to communicate a cryptic message. Its demeanour was serene yet disconcerting, and its featureless eyes seemed to bore into Jane's very soul.

Despite her escalating unease, Jane felt an inexplicable urge to document this enigmatic phenomenon further. She was driven as if by an invisible force, compelling her to capture more images of the spectral presence.

Days turned into weeks, and Jane's fixation intensified. The shimmering figure became an integral part of her daily life, appearing in every photograph she took in Short Heath—always concealed from the naked eye but unmistakably present in the world of the captured image.

As her obsession grew, Jane embarked on a quest to unveil the mystery of the shimmering spirit. She combed through local records and oral histories, searching for any hint of unusual occurrences or spectral apparitions in Short Heath.

To her astonishment, she discovered that her photographs were not the first evidence of the spectral presence. Long-forgotten tales recounted residents' encounters with fleeting, shimmering figures within their homes, accompanied by an inexplicable chill in the air.

The deeper Jane delved into Short Heath's history, the more evident the connection became. The spirit she had inadvertently captured through her lens appeared to be a silent guardian, a spectral protector of the neighbourhood, watching over its inhabitants from the shadows.

As Jane persisted in her photographic exploration of Short Heath, she began to sense the spirit's benign presence. A peculiar kinship developed between her and the shimmering figure, as if it had chosen her to be its keeper, disclosing itself solely through the medium of photography.

Over time, Jane's photographs of the shimmering spirit garnered attention, attracting visitors from near and far who were intrigued by the ethereal enigma. However, Jane remained cautious, ensuring that no tangible evidence of the spirit's presence was left behind. She knew that its existence was a well-kept secret, a mystery that would remain hidden.

As the years passed, Jane's life became inextricably intertwined with Short Heath's shimmering spirit. Her camera became a portal, a link between the living and the ethereal, a connection to the enigmatic world that existed just beyond perception.

In the heart of Short Heath, where each photograph concealed the spectral secret, Jane's unique bond with the shimmering spirit defied explanation. The neighbourhood's history was preserved not only in the structures themselves but also in the haunting, unseen images captured through Jane's lens—a silent testament to the hidden mysteries of the Black Country.

THE BLOXWICH BELLRINGER

In the charming town of Bloxwich, nestled amidst the rolling hills of the Black Country, a captivating legend played out—a tale that would forever bind two close friends in a web of mystery and intrigue.

Martin and Steven, lifelong companions whose friendship had weathered the test of time, had always been enamoured with the old church that graced their beloved town. Its ancient spire, adorned with weather-worn stones, stood as a sentinel against the inexorable march of the years. The heart of the town, it had witnessed generations come and go, its bells tolling in celebration and solace.

One crisp autumn evening, as the setting sun painted the sky in hues of amber and rose, Martin and Steven found themselves standing before the towering church. The splendour of the twilight cast an ethereal glow upon the centuries-old structure, and the town seemed to hush in reverence.

It was then, in the quiet of that sacred moment, that they heard it—the unmistakable tolling of the church bells. The sound resonated through the tranquil town, its melody at once hauntingly beautiful and undeniably supernatural.

As the last vestiges of daylight faded into darkness, the spectral chimes persisted, echoing through the cobblestone streets. Martin and Steven exchanged astonished glances, their eyes reflecting the bewilderment that coursed through their souls. They gazed up at the ancient belfry, but no living being met their searching eyes. Instead, the bell ropes swung with a spectral grace, pulled by unseen hands, their cadence orchestrating the eerie symphony that enveloped the town.

Martin and Steven had often spent their childhood exploring the nooks and crannies of the church, their curious spirits drawn to its history. They knew every corner of the grand edifice, from the hidden chambers to the winding staircases that led to the belfry.

Driven by curiosity and an indomitable friendship, they embarked on a quest to unravel the enigma of the Bloxwich Bellringer. Armed with determination, they climbed the dusty staircases, their footsteps echoing through the hollow halls.

When they reached the belfry, a shiver of anticipation ran down their spines. The bell ropes swung with an otherworldly grace, and the pealing of the bells reverberated through their souls. But the sight that greeted them was more astonishing than they could have ever imagined.

Amidst the ethereal, translucent mist that filled the belfry, they beheld the figure of a man—a spectral form with a serene countenance. He moved with a graceful fluidity, his movements synchronised with the bell's tolling.

Martin and Steven stood in awe as the phantom bell ringer continued his ethereal performance. His presence exuded a sense of purpose, as if he were carrying out a sacred duty that transcended the boundaries of the living.

In the ensuing weeks, Martin and Steven returned to the belfry time and again, forging an unspoken connection with the enigmatic bell ringer. They communicated not through words but through shared experiences, as if the spirit recognized their genuine intentions.

As the years passed, Martin and Steven embraced their unique bond with the Bloxwich Bellringer. They regarded him as a guardian spirit, a sentinel who protected their beloved town in moments of peril and celebrated its joys. The bell ringer became an integral part of their lives, a silent friend who shared their secrets and watched over their dreams.

In Bloxwich, where the bonds of friendship were deepened by the mysteries of the Black Country, Martin and Steven found solace in the knowledge that their connection to the supernatural had forged an unbreakable bond—one that would forever resonate through the town's hallowed streets.

Yet, amid the mystique of their relationship with the spectral bell ringer, a new chapter of the legend would soon unfold, casting a deeper shadow upon their lives. It was on a fateful, stormy night that the truth behind the ghostly tolling bells would be revealed, challenging the very fabric of their reality. The ancient church, the town, and the enigmatic spirit would all play a part in the most astonishing revelation they could ever imagine.

FORDHOUSES'
FLICKERING FLAME

In the heart of the Black Country, nestled amidst the labyrinthine streets of Fordhouses, a chilling legend lingered—a tale that whispered of the supernatural, a phenomenon that transcended time and reason.

John, a weary traveller with the weight of the world on his shoulders, had often heard murmurs of this eerie legend from the locals. They spoke of a mysterious light—a flickering flame that would manifest along the winding roads of Fordhouses on certain moonless nights. It was said that this spectral light could lead travellers astray, ensnaring them in an otherworldly dance that defied explanation.

One autumn evening, as the sun dipped below the horizon, casting long shadows across the worn cobblestone streets, John found himself standing at the crossroads of Fordhouses. Weariness clung to his bones, and he longed for nothing more than the comfort of his own home. But fate had other plans.

As the twilight deepened and the first stars began to twinkle in the ink-black sky, a soft, flickering light appeared at the edge of John's vision. It beckoned to him—a pale, ghostly flame that danced in the darkness. Its allure was undeniable, a siren's call that drew him closer with each step.

The night seemed to grow darker, and the world around John faded into obscurity, leaving only the flickering flame as his guide. He walked, his senses entranced by the spectral light, as it led him deeper into the labyrinth of Fordhouses.

The narrow streets twisted and turned, their cobblestones worn smooth by centuries of travellers who had ventured into the heart of this enigmatic town. The houses that lined the roads appeared abandoned, their windows dark and devoid of life. An eerie silence settled upon the town, broken only by the faint, ethereal humming of the flickering flame.

Time lost all meaning as John followed the ghostly light, his surroundings growing ever more unfamiliar. The buildings seemed to age and crumble before his eyes, as if he had stepped into another era—an era where Fordhouses had not yet known the ravages of industry.

As he journeyed deeper into the heart of this temporal enigma, John felt a profound sense of disorientation. It was as if the very fabric of reality had unravelled, and he had been cast adrift in a sea of time. The flickering flame, his only companion in this strange odyssey, danced on, its elusive nature defying comprehension.

Eventually, the light led John to a desolate square, surrounded by buildings that bore the scars of centuries. In the centre of the square, an ancient well stood—a relic of a bygone era. The flickering flame hovered above the well, its glow casting eerie shadows on the weathered stones.

As John approached the well, a sense of foreboding washed over him. He could feel the weight of history pressing down upon him, a reminder of the countless souls who had walked these same streets. It was then that he understood the true nature of the flickering flame—it was a guardian of time, a spectral sentinel that watched over the secrets of Fordhouses.

The flame's dance grew more frenetic, as if it sensed a presence beyond that of John's. It flickered and swirled, casting an otherworldly glow that bathed the square in an unearthly light. And then, in the heart of that luminous spectacle, John saw it—a fleeting glimpse of figures from another era.

Spectral forms materialised before him, the townsfolk of Fordhouses as they had once been. They moved with an ethereal grace, their garments of a bygone era billowing in the spectral breeze. They were laughing, dancing, and living their lives as if time had never passed.

John watched in awe as the past and present intertwined in this eerie spectacle. It was as if the flickering flame had bridged the gap between two worlds, allowing him to bear witness to a history long forgotten.

But as quickly as it had begun, the spectral vision faded, and the townsfolk of Fordhouses vanished into the mists of time. The flickering flame returned to its gentle dance, leading John back along the winding streets of the town.

As he emerged from the labyrinth of Fordhouses, John found himself standing at the crossroads once more. The spectral light, its purpose fulfilled, dissipated into the night, leaving him with a sense of wonder and awe.

In the Black Country, where the boundaries of time and reality blurred, John had experienced an encounter unlike any other. The flickering flame of Fordhouses had granted him a glimpse into a world long past, a testament to the enduring mysteries that lingered in the shadows of this enigmatic town. And as he continued his journey home, he carried with him the knowledge that Fordhouses would forever hold its secrets close, guarded by the spectral sentinel of the flickering flame.

THE PERTON
PHANTOM PIPER

The day was as ordinary as any other in Perton. The sun hung low on the horizon, casting long shadows that stretched across the quaint streets. Clive, a stoic man with a heart untouched by superstition, went about his daily routine without a care for the eerie legends that clung to his town.

Maria, on the other hand, had always been fascinated by the mysteries of the Black Country. She had a penchant for the supernatural, often finding solace in the eerie tales that echoed through the region. And on this particular evening, as twilight descended upon Perton, it was Maria who would embark on a journey that would forever alter her perception of the world.

As she walked along the cobblestone streets, her footsteps echoing in the quiet, Maria heard something that sent a shiver down her spine—an eerie, haunting melody that danced on the breeze. It was the ethereal sound of a bagpipe, its mournful tune winding its way into her very soul.

Clive, who had been strolling beside her, turned to Maria with a quizzical look. "Did you hear that, Maria?" he asked, his voice tinged with unease.

Maria nodded, her heart pounding with a mixture of excitement and trepidation. "Yes, Clive. It's the Perton Phantom Piper."

The legend of the Perton Phantom Piper had been whispered through generations. It was said that on certain moonless nights, the ghostly sound of a bagpipe could be heard echoing through the town, its haunting melody luring those who listened into the shadows.

As the spectral tune continued to play, Maria and Clive followed the ethereal sound, their curiosity getting the better of them. The melody led them through winding streets and narrow alleys until they found themselves in front of an old, abandoned building—a relic from Perton's past.

The building stood like a sentinel of time, its windows boarded up, and its walls weathered by the years. But it was here, amidst the decaying structure, that the haunting bagpipe melody seemed to emanate.

Maria and Clive exchanged uncertain glances, their hearts heavy with a sense of foreboding. Without a word, they pushed open the creaking door and stepped into the dimly lit interior.

The air was thick with the musty scent of decay, and the room was filled with relics of the past—an old table, dusty chairs, and faded photographs that lined the walls. But what drew their attention was the figure standing at the centre of the room—a spectral piper, his form translucent and otherworldly.

He played his bagpipes with an ethereal grace, his fingers moving deftly over the instrument's pipes. The haunting melody swirled around the room, filling the air with an otherworldly presence.

Maria and Clive watched in awe as the spectral piper continued his eerie performance. His eyes, though devoid of life, seemed to fixate on them with a haunting intensity. It was as if he was beckoning them to join in his spectral dance, to become a part of the timeless legend that had gripped Perton for generations.

As the last notes of the bagpipe's mournful tune faded into the darkness, the spectral piper slowly dissipated into thin air, leaving Maria and Clive alone in the abandoned building. The room was once again silent, its secrets veiled in the shadows.

They knew that the legend of the Perton Phantom Piper would persist, passed down through generations as a testament to the enduring mysteries of the Black Country. Maria and Clive had become a part of that legend, forever bound to the ghostly piper's haunting melody.

In Perton, where the line between the living and the supernatural was blurred, Maria and Clive had witnessed an enigma that defied explanation. The Perton Phantom Piper had granted them a glimpse into a world beyond the ordinary, a world where the boundaries of time and reality merged, and the haunting melodies of a bagpipe played on for eternity.

TIVIDALE'S TIMELESS TAVERN

In the heart of Tividale, amidst the bustling streets and dimly lit alleyways, there stood a quaint and unassuming tavern known as "The Whispering Tankard." Unlike any other establishment in the Black Country, it held a secret—a mysterious phenomenon that defied explanation and left patrons in a state of bewilderment.

Jamie, a seasoned traveller with a penchant for the peculiar, had heard whispers of this tavern and its enigmatic reputation. It was said that within the time-worn walls of "The Whispering Tankard," the past and present converged in a dance of spectral revelation.

One moonless night, as the town of Tividale lay shrouded in darkness, Jamie found himself drawn to the tavern's unassuming entrance. The tavern's sign creaked ominously in the chilly night breeze, and the flickering lanterns cast eerie shadows that seemed to beckon him closer.

The tavern's interior was warm and inviting, the low hum of conversation filling the air as patrons huddled around wooden tables, their faces bathed in the soft glow of candlelight. The bartender, a grizzled man with eyes that held the weight of centuries, poured drinks with practised ease.

Jamie found an empty stool at the bar, the creaking floorboards beneath him adding to the tavern's timeless ambiance. As he ordered a drink, he couldn't help but notice the curious glances exchanged between the patrons.

It was then that Jamie felt it—a subtle shift in the atmosphere, a tremor that seemed to vibrate through the very foundation of the tavern. The voices of the patrons grew hushed, and the air grew heavy with anticipation.

And then, as if guided by an unseen hand, Jamie's surroundings began to change. The dimly lit tavern faded away, replaced by a scene from a bygone era. The wooden beams overhead became polished oak, the patrons transformed into men and women in antiquated attire, and the flickering candles gave way to gas lamps that bathed the room in a soft, ethereal glow.

Jamie's heart quickened as he realised that he had been transported to the tavern's past, a witness to a moment frozen in time. The patrons of the bygone era continued their conversations, their voices a haunting echo of days long past.

As Jamie observed, he couldn't help but notice that the barkeep remained unchanged. His gaze met Jamie's across the centuries, and he nodded knowingly, as if he were the guardian of this temporal phenomenon.

Jamie watched in awe as the scene played out before him. The patrons laughed and shared stories, their faces illuminated by the warm glow of the gas lamps. It was as if he had stepped into a living, breathing painting—a glimpse into a world that had long since faded into the annals of history.

But just as suddenly as it had begun, the temporal shift reversed itself. The flickering gas lamps gave way to modern-day candles, the antique attire of the patrons reverted to contemporary clothing, and the hushed conversations returned to their previous volume.

As Jamie blinked in astonishment, he realised that he was once again in the present, seated at the same stool at the bar. The bartender regarded him with a knowing smile, as if he had seen this wonder unfold countless times before.

Wordlessly, Jamie finished his drink, paid his tab, and left "The Whispering Tankard." He knew that he had experienced something truly extraordinary—an encounter with the mysteries of time itself.

In Tividale, where the past and present converged within the walls of "The Whispering Tankard," Jamie had been granted a glimpse into a world beyond the ordinary. The tavern's secret remained, a timeless enigma that continued to bewitch those who dared to step through its unassuming doors—a place where history and the supernatural converged, and the whispers of the past echoed for those willing to listen.

WOMBOURNE'S
WEEPING WOMAN

In the area of Wombourne, where the dense woods cast long shadows that seemed to harbour ancient secrets, there existed a haunting tale that had been passed down through generations. It spoke of a sorrowful spirit known as the Weeping Woman, a spectre whose mournful presence had been witnessed by those brave enough to venture near the woods.

Brenda, a young woman with a fascination for the unknown and an insatiable curiosity, had heard whispers of the Weeping Woman since her childhood. The stories painted a picture of a ghostly figure, draped in tattered, ethereal garments, her dishevelled hair concealing a face eternally obscured by grief.

One mist-laden evening, as the sun dipped below the horizon, Brenda found herself drawn to the edge of the woods. The air grew heavy with the scent of damp earth and decaying leaves, and the woods seemed to beckon her forward.

It was then, in the depths of twilight, that Brenda heard it— the heart-wrenching sound of a woman weeping, her mournful sobs echoing through the stillness of the woods. Goosebumps prickled on Brenda's skin as she cautiously ventured deeper into the shadows.

The mournful wails grew louder, and Brenda's heart pounded in her chest. She moved with trepidation, guided by the eerie cries that seemed to emanate from the very heart of the woods. The dense canopy above filtered the fading light, casting an eerie pallor over her surroundings.

As Brenda pressed on, she stumbled upon a small, moonlit clearing. There, amid a carpet of moss and ferns, she beheld the spectral figure of the Weeping Woman. Clad in a tattered white gown, her long, dishevelled hair concealed her face, and her translucent form glowed in the ethereal light of the moon.

The Weeping Woman's grief was palpable—a sorrow that transcended the realm of the living. Her ghostly sobs wracked her spectral frame as she clutched a bundle of wilted flowers to her chest. Brenda watched in both awe and trepidation, her heart aching for the spirit's inexplicable torment.

Brenda dared not approach too closely, sensing the profound sorrow that emanated from the Weeping Woman. Instead, she remained hidden in the shadows, a silent observer of the spectral scene. The woods seemed to come alive with a mournful symphony, as if the very trees and leaves grieved alongside the forlorn spirit.

As the night deepened, Brenda continued to watch, her own emotions entwined with the Weeping Woman's sorrow. It was as if the ghostly figure mourned not only a lost love but the countless tragedies that had befallen the world.

Just before the first light of dawn, as the spectral figure's cries reached a crescendo, Brenda witnessed a flicker of movement within the woods. A phantom-like figure, indistinct yet somehow familiar, materialised from the shadows.

The Weeping Woman's spectral form turned towards the newcomer, her mournful wails subsiding into a hushed silence. For a fleeting moment, the two ghostly figures seemed to share an unspoken connection, their translucent forms bathed in the ghostly light of the moon.

With a final, heart-rending sob, the Weeping Woman slowly dissipated into the misty woods, her figure fading until she became one with the night. The phantom-like figure lingered for a moment longer, as if watching over the vanishing spirit, before also fading away into the depths of the forest.

Brenda remained in the clearing, profoundly moved by the ethereal encounter she had borne witness to. The memory of the Weeping Woman's mournful cries and the enigmatic presence that had appeared in the woods would forever haunt her dreams.

In Wombourne, where the woods concealed secrets that defied explanation, Brenda had glimpsed into the spectral realm, a world where grief and love transcended the boundaries of time and death. The Weeping Woman's lament echoed through the woods, a testament to the enduring power of sorrow and the mysteries that lingered in the heart of Wombourne's ancient woods.

THE MYSTERY OF
MERRY HILL

In the bustling Merry Hill shopping centre, where modernity and commerce reigned supreme, there lingered a mystery that defied explanation. Shoppers from all walks of life had, at some point, encountered figures dressed in outdated clothing, their presence both perplexing and disconcerting.

Erin and Francis, a young couple with an insatiable curiosity and a love for shopping, often visited Merry Hill to explore the labyrinthine corridors of retail outlets. On one fateful afternoon, as they roamed the brightly lit halls, they became aware of a peculiar atmosphere that seemed to descend upon the bustling shoppers.

It began with a whisper—a faint rustle of clothing and hushed voices that did not belong to the present day. Erin and Francis exchanged puzzled glances, their curiosity piqued by the incongruous sounds that surrounded them.

As they continued to stroll through the mall, they noticed something even more baffling. Figures dressed in clothing that appeared to be from a bygone era mingled among the shoppers. Men in top hats and tailcoats, women in hoop skirts and bonnets —these apparitions moved through the crowd with an air of detachment, as if they existed in a world of their own.

Erin and Francis discreetly followed one of these enigmatic figures, a man dressed in a three-piece suit from the Victorian era. His attire, complete with a pocket watch and polished leather shoes, stood in stark contrast to the modern-day shoppers.

The couple watched in astonishment as the man approached a storefront that seemed to no longer exist—a shop that had long been replaced by a contemporary boutique. He reached out to touch the display window, his gloved hand passing through the glass as if it were an illusion.

Intrigued and unnerved in equal measure, Erin and Francis approached the spot where the apparition had stood, but there was no sign of him. It was as if he had vanished into thin air, leaving behind only the lingering whispers of his presence.

Over the coming weeks, Erin and Francis returned to Merry Hill, each visit punctuated by eerie encounters with these time-displaced figures. They observed a woman from the Edwardian era perusing a digital storefront, a man in a bowler hat engrossed in a smartphone, and a Victorian family sitting on an invisible bench, laughing at a sight only they could see.

The sightings grew increasingly frequent, their appearances unpredictable and fleeting. Shoppers around Erin and Francis seemed oblivious to the apparitions, going about their business as if nothing were amiss.

One evening, as the couple roamed the deserted halls of Merry Hill after closing hours, they stumbled upon a spectral gathering. Figures from various eras stood in a circle, their ghostly forms illuminated by a faint, otherworldly light.

In the centre of the circle was a woman dressed in a lavish ball gown reminiscent of the Roaring Twenties. She twirled with grace, her laughter echoing through the empty corridors. Erin and Francis watched in awe as the spectral revelry unfolded before their eyes.

The figures seemed to exist in a realm that intersected with the shopping centre's reality—a time capsule that held a myriad of moments from the past. But their appearances were brief, and as dawn approached, they gradually faded away like fragments of a half-remembered dream.

Erin and Francis, though bewildered by the inexplicable phenomenon, felt a strange connection to these apparitions. It was as if they had become custodians of Merry Hill's mysterious secret—a portal to the past that emerged in the heart of a modern shopping centre.

As the couple left Merry Hill that morning, the memories of their encounters lingered like a lingering fragrance. In the bustling mall, where commerce thrived and the modern world reigned supreme, Erin and Francis had glimpsed into a timeless dimension—a place where the echoes of the past danced among the living, leaving behind only enigmatic whispers of history.

GHOSTLY GATHERINGS
OF GREAT BRIDGE

In Great Bridge, where the modern world intertwined with echoes of the past, there existed a sinister secret that had plagued the town's inhabitants for generations. The ghostly gatherings that occurred at certain times were no longer seen as quaint reenactments but as ominous spectacles that sent shivers down the spines of even the bravest souls.

Malcolm and Greg, lifelong residents of Great Bridge, had initially been intrigued by these eerie occurrences. However, as the gatherings grew more frequent and unsettling, their fascination gave way to dread. It was as if an ancient curse had awakened, and the apparitions were no longer content with their historical reenactments.

One moonless night, as the town lay shrouded in an unnatural silence, Malcolm and Greg ventured into the heart of Great Bridge. The cobblestone streets were dimly lit by flickering gas lamps, casting elongated shadows that seemed to stretch and twist like malevolent spirits.

As they reached the town square, their senses were assaulted by a palpable malevolence that hung in the air. The usual hushed conversations of the spectral figures had transformed into ominous murmurs, their gestures and expressions contorted with a sinister intent.

The apparitions, dressed in archaic attire, gathered in a foreboding circle. Their faces remained hidden in shadow, their laughter a chilling echo of joy long turned to madness. The soft, melancholic melody that accompanied their gatherings had morphed into a dissonant cacophony that grated on the nerves.

Malcolm and Greg watched in horrified fascination as the ghostly figures performed a grotesque and macabre dance. Their movements were frenzied and erratic, their spectral forms twisting and contorting as if possessed by some maleficent force.

The once-elegant woman from the Victorian era, whose presence had once held a touch of melancholy, now bore a malevolent glare. She reached out with spectral fingers, her touch sending a shock of icy dread through Malcolm and Greg's hearts.

The spectral orchestra, instead of serenading the dancers, played discordant notes that resonated with a sinister energy. The very ground beneath their feet seemed to tremble as if recoiling from the unholy spectacle.

Malcolm and Greg, their bravery fueled by desperation, dared to approach the ghastly gathering. As they drew closer, the ghostly figures turned their shadowed faces towards them. Hollow eyes, devoid of humanity, bore into their souls, and a guttural, inhuman chorus filled the air.

In a terrifying crescendo, the apparitions descended upon Malcolm and Greg, their unearthly shrieks tearing through the night. The friends, overwhelmed by a terror beyond description, fled from the town square, their hearts pounding in their chests.

From that night on, Malcolm and Greg dared not venture into the heart of Great Bridge. They became reclusive, haunted by the nightmarish vision of the spectral gathering that had taken a malevolent turn. The town's once-enigmatic secret had become a curse that loomed over their lives, a chilling reminder of the darkness that lurked within the heart of their beloved town.

In Great Bridge, where the past and present converged in a nightmarish dance, Malcolm and Greg had become prisoners of a sinister enigma. The ghostly gatherings were no longer a source of wonder but a haunting terror that would forever torment their souls, a nightmarish legacy that would endure for generations to come.

OAKHAM'S OMINOUS OWL

In the ancient town of Oakham, nestled amidst the mist-shrouded hills of the Black Country, there existed a chilling legend that had gripped the hearts of its inhabitants for generations. It was a tale of an ethereal owl—an ominous guardian that was said to watch over the town's oldest secrets.

Grace, a young woman with a curiosity that rivalled her fearlessness, had grown up hearing whispers of the mysterious owl. The stories painted a picture of an otherworldly creature, its presence an omen of impending doom and misfortune. The townsfolk regarded it with a mixture of dread and reverence, for they believed that the owl held knowledge of Oakham's deepest, darkest mysteries.

One moonless night, as the town lay veiled in an eerie silence, Grace found herself drawn to the town's oldest cemetery. The ancient tombstones stood like sentinels, their inscriptions faded with time, bearing witness to centuries of Oakham's history. The towering oak trees that surrounded the cemetery cast long, gnarled shadows, and the air was thick with an otherworldly stillness.

As Grace wandered deeper into the cemetery, she noticed a peculiar sensation—an unsettling feeling that she was being watched. She glanced up, her breath catching in her throat, and there, perched atop a moss-covered gravestone, was the ominous owl.

Its eyes, orbs of glistening onyx, bore into Grace's soul with an intensity that sent shivers down her spine. The owl's feathers were pure white, yet its presence exuded a sinister energy that seemed to defy the laws of nature.

Grace dared not move, her heart pounding in her chest as she locked eyes with the spectral creature. In that eerie silence, she felt as though the owl could peer into the depths of her being, reading her thoughts and secrets.

And then, with a haunting hoot that reverberated through the cemetery, the owl spread its wings and took flight. Grace watched in awe as it soared into the night sky, its form illuminated by the ethereal glow of the moon.

Determined to unravel the enigma of the ominous owl, Grace embarked on a quest to understand its significance. She delved into the town's history, poring over dusty archives and speaking to the eldest residents who held the town's most guarded tales.

What she discovered sent a chill down her spine. The owl, it seemed, had been a presence in Oakham for centuries, appearing at pivotal moments in the town's history—times of tragedy, war, and upheaval. It was said that those who encountered the owl would be marked by a dark fate, their lives forever entwined with Oakham's ominous secrets.

As Grace delved deeper into the mystery, she uncovered tales of vanished residents, unsolved mysteries, and unspoken curses. It seemed that the owl, with its unblinking gaze and chilling hoot, was a harbinger of the town's darkest truths.

One night, as Grace stood once again in the cemetery, she felt the ominous presence of the owl behind her. She turned slowly, her heart pounding, and there it was, perched on a gravestone, its eyes gleaming with an unholy knowledge.

The owl hooted once more, its sound a mournful dirge that echoed through the cemetery. And then, with a sudden and inexplicable force, it vanished into the night, leaving Grace with a sense of foreboding that chilled her to the core.

In Oakham, where the past and present converged in an

unsettling dance, Grace had become entangled in the enigma of the ominous owl. It was a guardian of the town's oldest secrets, a spectral sentinel that watched over Oakham's mysteries with unrelenting vigilance.

Grace knew that her quest was far from over, that the owl held knowledge that could change the course of Oakham's history. But as she stared into the darkness where the owl had disappeared, she couldn't help but wonder if some secrets were better left buried in the shadows.

THE MUSEUM'S
SILENT SOLDIER

In the depths of the Black Country, a region steeped in the industrial echoes of a bygone era, there lay a place of both reverence and trepidation—the Black Country Museum. This living museum stood as a sentinel against the relentless march of time, preserving the rich history of the region, capturing the essence of moments long past. But within its hallowed halls, beneath the watchful eyes of antique mannequins and within the confines of meticulously recreated streets, a spectral presence stirred—a silent World War I soldier who would nod respectfully to passersby before fading away into the mists of history.

Ruth, a devoted employee of the museum with an unquenchable curiosity, had heard whispers of the silent soldier since the day she first set foot within the museum's vintage world. The tales spoke of a spectral figure, clad in the uniform of a World War I soldier, who would materialise in the corners of the museum, his presence as ephemeral as a wisp of smoke. At first, these stories had seemed like nothing more than the product of overactive imaginations, the natural byproduct of working in a place so steeped in history. However, as Ruth would soon discover, the legends held a glimmer of truth.

One quiet afternoon, when the museum was bathed in the soft, dappled light filtering through mist-covered windows, Ruth embarked on her usual rounds. She strolled through the meticulously recreated streets, each step echoing through the empty alleyways. It was in the quietude that she felt an inexplicable chill in the air, an unsettling presence that raised the hairs on the back of her neck.

Turning a corner, her footsteps muffled by the vintage cobblestone beneath her, Ruth saw him—the silent soldier. He stood at attention, his eyes concealed beneath the shadow of his steel helmet, his uniform adorned with the medals of valour, and his boots polished to a gleam. The soldier's presence exuded a sense of solemn duty, a commitment that transcended the boundaries of time.

Ruth approached cautiously, her heart pounding as she realised she was in the company of a spectral figure from a war long past. Her eyes locked with those hidden behind the veil of history, and she was struck by the depth of sorrow they seemed to convey—a sorrow that bore witness to the horrors of a bygone era.

As if acknowledging her presence, the soldier nodded respectfully, a silent exchange of recognition. It was a moment that resonated deeply with Ruth, for she understood that this was no ordinary spectre. This was a sentinel of history, a guardian of memories, and a witness to the indomitable human spirit that had endured the trials of war.

The soldier's spectral form began to shift, a gradual transformation that blurred the lines between past and present. Ruth watched, her breath caught in her throat, as the museum's vintage streets and displays morphed into a war-torn battlefield. The air became heavy with the acrid scent of mud and fear, and the soldier remained steadfast amidst the chaos, a symbol of courage in the face of unimaginable horror.

As she observed, Ruth felt the weight of history pressing down upon her. The soldier's spectral companions, fellow soldiers from a bygone era, marched silently past. Their faces bore the scars of battle, their eyes haunted by memories that would never fade. Each step they took resonated with the echoes of a war that had forever changed the course of history.

The soldier's nod, once a silent greeting, now held the weight of a hundred stories left untold. He acknowledged Ruth with a sense of gratitude, as if her presence had bridged the gap between the past and the present. The soldier's eyes conveyed a solemn understanding, a shared acknowledgment of the sacrifices made in the name of duty and honour.

As the distant sounds of battle grew louder, the soldier began to fade, his form dissipating into the mists of time. Ruth stood alone in the recreated battlefield, the echoes of history reverberating in her soul. She knew that what she had experienced was a rare and profound encounter with the past— a connection forged through the silent soldier and his comrades.

In the Black Country Museum, where history and the supernatural converged, Ruth had walked in the footsteps of those who had served in the trenches of World War I. The soldier's salute had become a silent testament to the enduring spirit of those who had faced the horrors of war with unwavering courage.

Ruth continued her work in the living museum, tending to the exhibits that preserved the region's history. But in the quiet moments between the visitors and the echoes of the past, she carried with her the memories of the spectral soldiers and their stories. Their presence served as a reminder of the sacrifices made in the name of history, a tribute to the bravery of those who had served their country in its darkest hours.

As she looked out over the museum's vintage streets, Ruth knew that the silent soldier would return, for his duty was timeless—a sentinel of history, a guardian of memories, and a silent witness to the enduring human spirit. And as long as the museum stood, so too would the soldier, nodding respectfully to passersby and fading away into the mists of history, a symbol of honour and remembrance.

THE BEWDLEY BRIDGE
BANSHEE

The Black Country, a land steeped in industrial history and folklore, there existed a bridge that had endured centuries of whispered tales and spine-chilling legends. This bridge, known to locals as the Bewdley Bridge, had become the canvas upon which an unsettling tale of the supernatural was painted—a tale of the enigmatic Bewdley Bridge Banshee. Her haunting wail had echoed through generations, particularly on fog-draped nights when the boundary between the living and the dead seemed to blur and waver.

Dave and Brad, lifelong friends who shared a fascination with the eerie and the unexplained, had been regaled with stories of the Banshee's chilling cries from a tender age. The tales spun a narrative of a spectral figure, a woman draped in tattered white robes, who would materialise on the bridge when the veil of fog descended upon the land. Her scream, it was said, could pierce the very soul of anyone unlucky enough to hear it.

One mist-laden evening, as the moon loomed low in the heavens, Dave and Brad felt themselves inexorably drawn to the Bewdley Bridge. The fog enshrouded the landscape like a spectral cloak, casting an eerie hush upon the world. It was a silence that seemed to hold its breath, as if anticipating the mournful cry of the Banshee that lingered in the air like a whispered omen.

Standing at the precipice of the bridge, their breath visible in the crisp night air, the two friends gazed upon the tranquil river below. Its surface mirrored the ethereal mist that danced around, creating a dreamlike reflection of the world above. As they peered into the veiled distance, the hairs on the napes of their necks stood on end, as if anticipating a revelation.

It was at that moment they heard it—a distant, otherworldly scream that sent shivers cascading down their spines. The sound, as if born from the very heart of the fog, carried with it an unfathomable sense of sorrow and loss, echoing across the ages.

Dave and Brad exchanged apprehensive glances, their eyes wide with fear. The Banshee's cry intensified, drawing nearer with each passing heartbeat. It was as though the very fabric of reality was fraying at the edges, and they were ensnared in an ancient, supernatural lament.

Slowly, the figure of a woman began to materialise amidst the mist. She wore robes so white they seemed to shimmer with spectral light, her hair whipped into a chaotic frenzy by an unseen tempest. Her eyes, pools of unfathomable darkness, bore into their souls with a profound intensity. The Banshee had arrived.

With a heart-rending scream that sent tremors through their beings, the Banshee raised her arms heavenward. Her unearthly voice carried a haunting melody, a dirge that permeated the fog-choked night. Dave and Brad felt a crushing weight of sorrow descend upon them, as if they had been submerged in the agony of centuries long past.

As they stood in a mesmerised blend of awe and terror, the Banshee's spectral form drifted closer to the bridge. Her mournful wail enveloped them, an ethereal symphony that transcended the confines of time itself, telling tales of ancient tragedies and unforgotten sorrows.

Dave and Brad, powerless to do anything but stand frozen in place, watched as the Banshee glided past them. Her eyes locked with theirs, and in that bone-chilling moment, they felt as though they were peering into the abyss of eternity itself. Her presence seemed to stretch back through the annals of history, an eternal witness to countless sorrows, a harbinger of doom.

Then, as abruptly as she had materialised, the Banshee began to fade. Her spectral form dissolved into the dissipating mist, her mournful wail growing ever fainter with each passing second. The fog gradually lifted, and the world returned to a semblance of normalcy.

Dave and Brad found themselves standing alone on the Bewdley Bridge, their hearts still racing from the otherworldly encounter. The Banshee had come and gone, leaving them with a profound sense of wonder and dread that would linger within them for the rest of their lives.

In the Black Country, where the realms of legend and reality frequently intertwined, Dave and Brad had borne witness to the Bewdley Bridge Banshee—an ephemeral figure whose cry of grief and loss echoed across the ages. They understood that her haunting presence would forever be etched into their memories, serving as a stark reminder of the enigmas that lurked in the fog-shrouded corners of the world and the chilling stories whispered from generation to generation.

PATTINGHAM'S
PACING PRIEST

In the quiet village of Pattingham, nestled amidst the tranquil embrace of the Black Country, there existed a spectral enigma that had long held the residents in its eerie grip—a ghostly clergyman whose apparition could be seen eternally pacing the path to what seemed to be an unfinished mission.

Harold, an elderly resident of Pattingham, had grown up with the unsettling tales of the Pacing Priest whispered by the village's elder folks. The stories spoke of a spectral figure, a clergyman in vestments as ancient as time itself, who would manifest along the winding path that led to the village church. His apparition was a sombre one, a testament to a mission left incomplete, and his footsteps echoed through the village's collective memory like a chilling dirge.

One moonless night, as the village lay shrouded in the embrace of darkness, Harold found himself drawn to the churchyard. The ancient stones and gnarled trees cast eerie shadows, and the night air was heavy with an unsettling stillness. The Pacing Priest had called to him, and he couldn't resist its eerie summons.

As Harold approached the churchyard, he felt the temperature drop, and an otherworldly chill crept down his spine. The moon, obscured by thick clouds, offered no solace, and the world seemed to hold its breath.

There, on the path leading to the church, Harold beheld the spectral figure of the Pacing Priest. The clergyman's attire was from a bygone era, his robe flowing with ethereal grace. His head was bowed, and his hands clasped a tattered prayer book. Each step he took resonated with an eerie cadence, echoing through the night like a mournful heartbeat.

Harold watched in silence as the clergyman continued his eternal journey, his eyes cast downward, his face etched with an expression of profound solemnity. The weight of an unfinished mission hung about him like an invisible shroud, and Harold could sense the priest's sorrow.

As if sensing Harold's presence, the Pacing Priest raised his head. His eyes, orbs of mournful wisdom, met Harold's gaze, and the elderly man felt an inexplicable connection—a bond forged through time and circumstance.

The clergyman's spectral form began to shimmer, and the world around Harold began to change. The village church, with its crumbling spires and ivy-covered walls, transformed into a place of vibrant life—a thriving community hub where villagers gathered in joyous celebration.

Harold watched in astonishment as the scene played out before him. The Pacing Priest, now a living clergyman, led a congregation in prayer. His voice, filled with fervour and devotion, echoed through the church, and the villagers gathered around him seemed touched by an otherworldly grace.

Among the congregation, Harold noticed a young woman named Margaret. Her eyes shone with a radiant light, and her smile warmed his heart. Beside her stood a mischievous young boy named Louie, his laughter ringing through the church like a bell.

As Harold observed, he realised that he was witnessing a moment of profound significance—the completion of the clergyman's unfinished mission. The village, once plagued by hardship and sorrow, had found solace and joy through his guidance.

But just as suddenly as it had begun, the scene shifted. The village church reverted to its dilapidated state, and the living congregation transformed into spectral figures. The Pacing Priest, now back in his ghostly form, continued his eternal vigil, his footsteps echoing through the night.

Harold stood alone in the churchyard, his heart heavy with the weight of what he had witnessed. The Pacing Priest had shown him a glimpse of the past, a moment of fulfilment and purpose that had eluded him in life. And yet, for reasons unknown, he remained bound to the earthly realm, eternally pacing the path to his unfinished mission.

In Pattingham, where the spectral and the living coexisted in an eerie dance, Harold had been granted a haunting revelation —a testament to the enduring presence of those who sought to fulfil their purpose, even beyond the boundaries of life and death. The Pacing Priest's eternal vigil served as a reminder that some missions could never truly be completed, and their echoes lingered on, eternally haunting the village's collective memory.

THE DRAYTON DREAMER

In the small town of Drayton, nestled within the heart of the Black Country, an eerie phenomenon had woven its enigmatic web—the recurring dream of a guiding spirit showing residents unknown parts of their town. This spectral occurrence had gripped the town's residents, filling their nights with an unsettling sense of curiosity and dread.

Sarah, a young woman with an insatiable thirst for the mysteries of the unknown, had become aware of this phenomenon through hushed whispers and cautious glances exchanged between her fellow townspeople. The stories spoke of a spectral figure, a shadowy entity that would appear in the dreams of the town's inhabitants, leading them on nocturnal journeys to undiscovered corners of Drayton.

One moonless night, as Sarah lay in her bed, she felt an unexplainable drowsiness settle over her. The room grew darker, and a sensation of weightlessness washed over her. She realised that she was slipping into a dream, and her heart quickened with anticipation and trepidation.

In her dream, she found herself standing at the edge of a dimly lit alley, its cobblestone path shrouded in shadows. The chill in the air sent a shiver down her spine, and the only source of light was a flickering lantern that cast eerie, dancing silhouettes on the walls.

And then, emerging from the darkness, she saw it—a spectral figure cloaked in tattered robes, its face obscured by the hood of its garment. It beckoned to her with a ghostly hand, and Sarah felt an irresistible compulsion to follow.

As she ventured deeper into the alley, the spectral figure led her through a labyrinthine network of narrow passages and hidden courtyards, each more mysterious than the last. The town of Drayton revealed itself in a new and unfamiliar light, as if the dream had unveiled hidden layers of history and secrets.

Sarah's heart pounded with a mixture of fear and fascination as she followed the spectral guide. The dream felt strangely vivid, and the details of the town's hidden corners were etched into her memory with an eerie precision.

After what seemed like hours, the spectral guide brought her to a decaying mansion at the edge of town. Its grandeur had faded, and the once-majestic structure now stood in silent decay, its windows shattered and its walls covered in ivy.

The guide's spectral hand pointed to the mansion's entrance, and Sarah felt a sense of foreboding. With a heavy heart, she ventured inside, the creaking floorboards echoing through the empty halls.

As she explored the mansion's dark and winding corridors, she began to uncover fragments of a tragic story—a story of love and loss, of a family torn apart by secrets buried within these very walls.

In the depths of the mansion, she encountered another dreamer, Lucy, who shared her sense of curiosity and trepidation. Together, they delved deeper into the mansion's mysteries, each room revealing a new chapter of the tragic tale.

And then, as they reached the mansion's hidden basement, they uncovered the truth—a hidden chamber filled with old letters, photographs, and a crumbling journal. These artefacts told the story of Julie, a young woman who had once lived within these walls, her love affair with a mysterious stranger, and the tragic end that had befallen them both.

As the dream faded and Sarah awoke, she felt a profound sense of connection to the town's history, as if the dream had woven a tapestry of forgotten stories and long-lost souls. She knew that she had witnessed something beyond the ordinary, a glimpse into the mysteries that lay hidden beneath the surface of Drayton.

In Drayton, where dreams and reality blurred into a surreal tapestry, Sarah had experienced the enigma of the Drayton Dreamer—a guiding spirit that had led her, and others, on a haunting journey through the town's forgotten past. The dreams persisted, an eternal invitation to explore the mysteries that dwelled within the shadows of Drayton's history, beckoning those who dared to uncover its secrets.

FALLINGS PARK'S FADING FOOTPRINTS

In the area of Fallings Park, a quiet neighbourhood nestled amidst the sprawling Black Country, there was an uncanny phenomenon that haunted the long, dark winter nights—a mystery that defied explanation and sent shivers down the spines of its residents. This eerie enigma took the form of elusive footprints, which would appear and vanish in the freshly fallen snow, leaving behind an unsettling trail of intrigue.

Jasmine, a curious and intrepid soul, had encountered these enigmatic footprints firsthand. It was an especially frigid evening when she peered out of her frost-etched window to behold the peculiar sight—a series of footprints, appearing as if from nowhere, etched upon the pristine canvas of freshly fallen snow in her backyard.

The snowfall had been relentless, blanketing the world in a serene, white shroud. Yet, these footprints seemed untouched by the elements. Jasmine watched in bafflement as they meandered aimlessly through her yard, seemingly leading to nowhere and no one. Each impression was crisp and well-defined, as if they had been left mere moments ago, but there was no sign of any living soul nearby.

It was as though an invisible traveller had passed through her yard, their presence known only through these ethereal footprints. Jasmine's unease deepened as she noticed that the prints seemed to grow fainter with each passing moment, as if they were gradually fading away.

Over the course of the winter, the mysterious footprints became a recurring phenomenon. They would materialise in the midst of a snowfall, weaving intricate paths across lawns and streets, only to vanish into thin air before the eyes of those who chanced upon them.

Jasmine wasn't the only one who had been visited by these enigmatic imprints. Her friend Gail, who lived a few houses down, had her own eerie encounter. One particularly chilly evening, as Gail gazed out of her window at the fresh layer of snow that coated her garden, she gasped in astonishment.

There, imprinted in the snow, were the unmistakable outlines of footprints—small, delicate prints as if belonging to a child. Gail, knowing that her home was empty and that no children played nearby, felt a shiver of trepidation. She hurried outside, her breath forming misty clouds in the frigid air, but found no one in sight.

As she examined the footprints up close, Gail realised that they, too, were growing fainter by the second. It was as though the very snow beneath them was swallowing them whole, erasing any trace of their existence.

Jasmine and Gail would often discuss these eerie encounters, sharing their bewilderment and fear. The entire neighbourhood had become entranced by the elusive footprints that defied all logic. Theories abounded, from spectral visitors to echoes of long-lost souls, but none could truly explain the chilling phenomenon.

It wasn't just the appearance and disappearance of the footprints that unnerved the residents of Fallings Park. It was the unshakeable feeling that they were being watched, that unseen eyes observed their every move. The sense of being visited by a presence beyond the veil of the living weighed heavily on their minds.

As winter continued its icy grip on Fallings Park, the mysterious footprints became a spectral tapestry woven into the fabric of their lives. Each new occurrence brought with it a mixture of fascination and dread, as neighbours gathered to witness the uncanny event.

And then, one fateful night, as a dense snowfall blanketed the neighbourhood in a pristine white silence, Jasmine and Gail stood in Jasmine's backyard, their breath forming frosty clouds in the cold air. The footprints had returned, more intricate and bewildering than ever before.

The prints meandered in a labyrinthine pattern, as if tracing the steps of a spectral dance. They crossed and overlapped, forming an intricate design that seemed to defy all reason. Jasmine and Gail watched in awe and terror as the footprints twisted and turned, leading to a central point in the yard.

And there, in the midst of this spectral tapestry, a single word had been meticulously spelled out in footprints—an eerie message from the otherworldly visitor. The word was "FOLLOW."
Jasmine and Gail exchanged fearful glances. It was a message that sent shivers down their spines, a command from an unseen presence that beckoned them to uncover the secrets hidden within the enigmatic footprints.

As they hesitated, torn between curiosity and fear, a chill swept through the air, and the footprints began to fade, their delicate impressions melting into the snow. The word "FOLLOW" vanished before their eyes, leaving no trace behind.

The two friends stood alone in the icy silence, pondering the inexplicable message. They knew that the mystery of Fallings Park's fading footprints was far from over, and that they were now entangled in a web of enigma that would lead them on a journey through the chilling unknown.

In the heart of Fallings Park, where the line between the

living and the spectral grew thin, Jasmine and Gail had become witnesses to a phenomenon that defied explanation. The enigmatic footprints, appearing and vanishing like ghostly whispers in the snow, held the promise of uncovering secrets that lay hidden in the winter's embrace. The chilling mystery had taken root in their lives, and they could not deny its spectral call to "FOLLOW" wherever it may lead.

AFTERWORD

My journey through the heart of the Black Country, in search of its enigmatic and spine-tingling ghost stories, has been nothing short of an extraordinary odyssey. "50 Black Country Ghost Stories" represents the culmination of years of exploration, investigation, and an unrelenting passion for unravelling the mysteries that shroud this historically rich and haunted region.

Throughout these pages, I've had the privilege of sharing with you a glimpse into the spectral tapestry that blankets the Black Country—a land that I've come to regard as one of the most paranormally active in the world. Its coal mines, factories, canals, and streets have borne witness to countless tales of the unexplained, each a testament to the enduring and often haunting legacy of this industrial heartland.

From the enigmatic "Brierley Hill's Haunting Hymn," where the boundaries between life and death blur, to the ominous "Oakham's Ominous Owl," guardian of ancient secrets, this collection represents a diverse and chilling array of encounters with the supernatural. These stories are not merely a chronicle of eerie events but a reflection of the indomitable spirit of those who have lived and worked in this remarkable region.

As I reflect on my own experiences as a paranormal investigator, I'm struck by the profound impact the Black Country has had on my understanding of the unknown. It is a place where history lingers in the air, where the past reaches out to touch the present, and where the line between reality and the paranormal is often perilously thin.

But what is it about the Black Country that makes it such a magnet for the inexplicable and the supernatural? Some might argue that the echoes of the region's industrial past, with its tales of gruelling labour, hardship, and sacrifice, have left an indelible mark on the collective psyche of its residents. Others might posit that the very landscape itself, scarred by the remnants of industry, holds a unique resonance with the supernatural.

In my years of research and investigation, I've found that the Black Country's ghost stories share certain common threads. There is often a sense of history repeating itself, of past tragedies leaving an indelible imprint on the present. There is also a palpable connection to the land itself, as if the very earth beneath our feet holds the memories and spirits of those who once toiled and suffered here.

Yet, for all the eerie encounters and spine-chilling tales, the Black Country is also a place of resilience, community, and hope. It's a place where people have faced adversity with unwavering determination, where families have forged bonds that transcend the bounds of time, and where the human spirit has triumphed over darkness.

As I've delved into the stories contained within this book, I've been struck by the resilience and courage of the individuals who have encountered the supernatural. Whether it's the steadfast resolve of the "The Museum's Silent Soldier" witness, the quiet acceptance of the "Drayton Dreamer" dreamers, or the insatiable curiosity of those drawn to the "Fallings Park's Fading Footprints," each story is a testament to the human spirit in the face of the unknown.

It's important to remember that the tales within these pages are not just stories; they are experiences that have left an indelible mark on those who have lived them. The witnesses, whether through their fear, awe, or curiosity, have become part of the ongoing narrative of the Black Country's paranormal tapestry.

As I look back on my own journey, I am reminded that the

pursuit of the paranormal is not merely about seeking answers to age-old questions; it is about embracing the mysteries of the universe, wherever they may lead. The Black Country has offered me countless opportunities to explore the unknown, to bear witness to the unexplained, and to connect with those who share a deep fascination with the supernatural.

In closing, I want to express my gratitude to the people of the Black Country, whose willingness to share their stories and experiences has made this book possible. I am continually inspired by your openness and resilience in the face of the unexplained.

To the readers, I offer my thanks for embarking on this eerie journey through the Black Country's haunted history. May these stories linger in your thoughts, spark your curiosity, and leave you with a profound sense of wonder about the world that lies beyond the veil of the everyday.

As I continue my investigations and explorations, I remain dedicated to uncovering the enigmatic and the unexplained, and I look forward to sharing more tales of the Black Country's ghostly encounters in the future.

Until then, may your nights be filled with both dreams and the delicious chill of the unknown.

Sincerely,

Lee Brickley

ABOUT THE AUTHOR

Lee Brickley

Lee Brickley is an investigator and author with more than 35 titles currently in publication covering a broad range of subjects including true crime, ancient history, the paranormal, and more.

Born in England, Brickley has been a professional writer for more than two decades. He regularly features in the media due to wide interest in his work, and he has made numerous TV appearances.

BOOKS BY THIS AUTHOR

Lee Brickley's Paranormal X-Files

Click link for the entire series, including Lee's best-selling books on Cannock Chase

Printed in Great Britain
by Amazon

29592051R00097